CHICAGO PUBLIC LIBRARY

R00847 68143

C0-DXA-280

LB 2831.826 .I4 V37 1990

Varghese, Mariamma A.

Women administrators in education.

JUN 2 5 1992

$22.50

SOCIAL SCIENCES AND HISTORY DIVISION
SOCIAL SCIENCES DIVISION
CHICAGO PUBLIC LIBRARY
400 SOUTH STATE STREET
CHICAGO, IL 60605

© THE BAKER & TAYLOR CO.

WOMEN ADMINISTRATORS IN EDUCATION

Women Administrators
in Education

Mariamma A. Varghese

Distributed By
ADVENT BOOKS
141 East 44 Street
New York, NY 10017

HAR-ANAND PUBLICATIONS
in association with
VIKAS PUBLISHING HOUSE PVT LTD

VIKAS PUBLISHING HOUSE PVT LTD
576 Masjid Road, Jangpura, New Delhi - 110014

COPYRIGHT © Mariamma A. Varghese, 1990

All rights reserved. No part of this publication may be reproduced in any form without the prior written permission of the publishers.

Printed at
Mahalaxmi Press
96/1, Rashid Market, Delhi-51

Foreword

Equality between sexes has been constitutionally mandated. However, it can hardly be said to be a reality. Women's access to education at all levels remains extremely limited and, therefore, women's participation in the paid employment which is correlated with educational attainments is also very low. It is a fact that women's participation in modern sector is confined only to a narrow range of activities, like teaching, nursing, clerical, stenographic etc. Within the teaching profession there are very few women professors and readers. This is the situation not only in India but also in western countries, like UK, USA and European countries. Very few women enter management and they tend to perform jobs which are less visible. In this context, two major dimensions of the problems confronting women managers are: less number of women going for managerial jobs and those who do opt for this sphere face difficulties in entering and then succeeding in it. There are also stereo-types regarding woman managers, namely, that they absent themselves from work more often than males, they cannot handle crisis and so on. It is in this context that a study of woman managers in various fields is necessary so that the popular misconceptions are countered. Mrs. Varghese's study on Women Administrators in Education is, therefore, most welcome.

Prof. M.A. Varghese is a distinguished Educationist having had a varied experience in management of education at M.S. University, Baroda, Jadavpur University, Calcutta, and now at S.N.D.T. Women's University. The book coming from such a distinguished Educationist has a stamp of authenticity. The objectives of the study were threefold:

(i) To examine the perception of the administrators in education in relation to the process of management.
(ii) To identify the factors associated with the differences in the perception and managerial problems.
(iii) To examine the implications of the results for further development of management courses in education sector.

The study is based on interview with 100 Educational administrators out of a list of 200 administrators obtained from Bombay University and S.N.D.T. University. Thirty-five were male and 65 were women. The sample consisted of more men as senior administrators in relation to women who were in the middle and lower levels of management. Interview schedule focussed on several aspects, like management goals and aspirations, stresses and strains, motivation for work and costs and benefits of work. The study highlights the constraints faced by women in the management process, especially the interaction between career and married life. The study shows that there are no significant differences between men and women once they reach the level of senior administrators. Both men and women are capable and have the potential for effective management. However, considering the special constraints faced by women administrators, the study suggests several measures at the individual, family, organisational and at the government level. The study refers to the need for a policy decision regarding equivalent women's positions to men's positions, especially because some women have necessarily to work on part-time basis.

The findings and recommendations of the study would be widely welcome by the policy planners both in the public sector and the private sector. While the erudition brought to bear on the writing of the report and the data marshalled leave very little to be desired, I would like to mention a few points for putting the findings of the report in proper

Foreword

perspective. Admittedly, the scope of the study is limited being confined to women administrators in education. Administration or management is a rich field with many facets and for getting a rounded view, it is necessary to consider the position of women administrators and managers in several areas. My attention has been invited to a study done by Dr. Mary Joseph Louis of the Mother Theresa Women's University, Kodaikanal which deals with background and status of women executives in a variety of fields, including industry, commerce, banking, government administration, education administration etc.. One of the findings of this latter study is that interest in material gains is least among bank executives followed by doctors, and it is maximum among the school executives. Again regarding the ability to keep home and profession separate, bank executives lead followed by doctors, social welfare excutives and executives of higher education. This ability is least in the case of school executives. I am mentioning these findings to point out that many more such studies are required and a comparative view of women administrators in different areas needs to be taken before we can feel confident to make firm policy recommendations. The findings of Mother Theresa University study could be contested but they should serve as an reminder that different areas of administration have their own characteristics which would affect the performance of women administrators in those fields. The studies to be more meaningful, need to be on parallel male-female basis so that the specific problems from the point of view of women administrators can be pin-pointed.

The National Policy on Education refers to the objective of education for women's equality and for that purpose the need for empowerment of women. More recently the government have formulated a national perspective plan for women development. Administration and management are atleast partly a matter of power and I have no doubt that this study of "Women Administrators in Education" would be a link, in the chain which needs to be forged, for giving power to women.

I congratulate Mrs. Verghese for authoring this excellent

book and would like to commend it very warmly to all those who have interest of women's development and, therefore, national development at heart.

ABID HUSSAIN
*India's Ambassador
to the United States*

Preface

Education for women has been identified as the major instrument for development in developing countries. In the context of the cultural traditions, it has become necessary to make a woman aware of her personhood and enable her to have a liberated life. Education is to be used as the most potent instrument to enrich her to possess and exercise optimal power. During the International Women's Decade, the studies undertaken by various researchers proved that the discrimination women suffer from, are man-made and women have a rich potential in terms of purposeful action, management sense, endurance in difficulties, a will that is strong and the capacity to tackle crisis. However, for women to enter the professional arena and attain equality with men, appropriate professional training has to be extended and the same should be availed by them. In this context, it is important to create a suitable structure and climate for women to achieve professional competency and equality.

In order to perform the managerial role effectively, one has to understand the process of management, the leadership role and the factors affecting management of educational organisations. There is need for training in the various managerial skills and techniques relevant for our educational system.

The National Policy on Education emphasizes promotion of women's education in all areas of learning to eliminate any sex based stereotyping. With the acceptance of gender equality in the constitution, the plan of action should be simple. However, in the implementation stage, many obstacles creep in which directly or indirectly affect women's participation in education and in occupation. In India, the problems women face have a specific coloring depending on the socio-economic-cultural milieu in which she has been nurtured and moulded. Little consideration is given for providing opportunities for personality development. Many of them are not exposed to an environment congenial for effective development. When a woman is exposed to the macro environment the requirements to interact in specific situations facilitate her personality development and confidence.

This study on Women Administrators has been undertaken to understand the demands and constraints placed on women administrators and the perceptions of the process of management, which has thrown light on the lacunae in the training for women administrators in education. In training women for management in education, one needs to develop the decision making ability, confidence and assertiveness, besides the management techniques, financial management, team building and leadership roles. If more women have to succeed in educational administration, there are some essential considerations to be made at the governmental, organisational, technological individual and family level which are discussed in great detail in the book.

This research project was a collaborative research with the Education Management Department at Sheffield City Polytechnic, U.K. Similar study has been done in Sheffield which shows similarities and differences in the context of cultural differences. The author is particularly grateful to the Women's Research Unit, S.N.D.T. Women's University for extending financial support in undertaking this study and Jamuna Rani for preparing this manuscript. The suggestions incorporated in the book, I hope, would be useful for policy makers, teachers and administrators of education management.

Prof. M.A. Varghese

Contents

Chapters

1. **INTRODUCTION**   15-29
    1.1 Women and Education
    1.2 Women and Work
    1.3 Familial Role Constraints
    1.4 Sex Discrimination
    1.5 Sex Differences
    1.6 Facilitating Factors
    1.7 Women in Managerial Positions
    1.8 Objectives

2. **METHODOLOGY**   30-33

3. **FINDINGS**   34-109
    3.1 Perception of Educational Administrators in Relation to the Process of Management
    3.2 Administrator's Time Management
    3.3 Management Effectiveness
    3.4 Administrative Tasks
    3.5 Work Profile
    3.6 Home and Social Arena
    3.7 Impact of Career on Marriage
    3.8 Administrative Traits
    3.9 Perception about Women Administrators
    3.10 Problems of Administrators

4. **CONCLUSION**   110-121
    4.1 Implications for Training

Bibliography   122-125

Figures

Fig. 1. Level of Direction in Management
Fig. 2. Perceptions of the "requirements for delegation, the actual status" and differentials for men and women administrators
Fig. 3. Perceptions of the administrators regarding the requirements for delegation, actual status and differentials
Fig. 4. Organisational goal orientation of administrators
Fig. 5. Personal goal orientation of administrators
Fig. 6. Task orientation level of administrators
Fig. 7. Time allocation for administrative tasks
Fig. 8. Management of effectiveness and type of family
Fig. 9. Management effectiveness and family life cycle
Fig. 10. Management effectiveness and management outlook
Fig. 11. Management effectiveness and subordinate boss relationship
Fig. 12. Management effectiveness and the extent of interaction with the team
Fig. 13. Management effectiveness and power delegation
Fig. 14. Management effectiveness and power invested in the administrator
Fig. 15. Management effectiveness and task orientation
Fig. 16. Characteristics of men and women administrators on the following: 1. Confidence, 2. Aggresiveness, 3. Decisiveness, 4. Competitiveness, 5 Temperamental, 6. Efficiency, 7. Rationality, 8. Sensitive to negative signal, 9. Capacity for hardwork, 10. Honesty, 11. Sincerity, 12. Creativity
Fig. 17. Qualities required for an administrator
Fig. 18. Perception about women administrators
Fig. 19. There is no discrimination against women in educational administration
Fig. 20. Women are well represented in higher education
Fig. 21. Educational administration attracts able women because it is a respectable career
Fig. 22. Educational administration continues with marriage and family better than most careers
Fig. 23. Educational administration is poorly paid compared to other professions

Figures

Fig. 24. "There is equal pay for men and women in the same educational administrative positions."
Fig. 25. "Men dislike working for women administrators."
Fig. 26. "Women dislike working for women administrators."
Fig. 27. "Women disklike working for men administrators."
Fig. 28. "A limited number of positions available to women for administrative jobs"
Fig. 29. "It is difficult to keep good working relationship with female bosses"
Fig. 30. "The employee morale is affected to a great extent with women administrators"
Fig. 31. "Employee efficiency is affected to a great extent with women administrators"
Fig. 32. "Women rarely expect or want position of authority"
Fig. 33. "Women generally lack the (confidence) skills and training needed for a manager's job"
Fig. 34. "Women have to be exceptionally good to succeed as good administrators"
Fig. 35. "Women of today want to make a contribution to the organisation through position of authority"
Fig. 36. "Women lack ability in achieving equality in leadership"
Fig. 37. "Working has become a necessity in women's life"
Fig. 38. Women cannot be thought of in any other role than wife and mother by many people
Fig. 39. Women do not have the opportunity for mobility if need arises
Fig. 40. Women do not have an equal chance to succeed as administrators because of the constraints placed on her at home
Fig. 41. Women do not have an equal chance to succeed as administrators because of the constraints placed around her by the environment by virtue of her age
Fig. 42. Men and women should follow the same career paths if their capabilities are equal
Fig. 43. Women find less opportunities for advancement in educational institutions
Fig. 44. Women are socialised to carry out household duties and therefore would be incompetent in administrative positions

Chapter 1

Introduction

1.1 Women and Education

In India education for women has been identified as the major instrument for the development. The impact of women on themselves, their family and society cannot be over emphasised. The contribution women can make towards economic development of families as micro unit of the social system and also to the economic system through productive labour need to be monetarily assessed to understand the impact of women's education. With the acceptance of gender equality in the constitution, the principle of equality of access to the education for women was accepted by the national planners. The following table provides stagewise enrolment of girls in terms of percentage of total enrolment in higher education between 1970-1971 and 1981-82. In terms of total percentage at all levels of higher education, enrolment of girls improved steadily over the decade. [Table 1]

The sex ratio in enrolment in major faculties in higher education during the decade 1970 to 71 and 1980 to 81 shows that the percentage in the faculties of arts and science education has steadily increased over the decade. A statewise picture in percentage distribution of women teachers at different stages of school education obtained from the 5th round shows an all-round improvement so far as women teachers are concerned as shown in Table 2.

On the whole, women hold a small percentage of administrative positions although they constitute about 30% in the teaching profession in India. Mukherjee (1972) in his report

Table 1

Stagewise Girls Enrolment to the Total Enrolment in Higher Education in Percentage

Year	Graduate	Post-graduate	Research	Diploma	Total
1970-71	21.70	25.00	20.70	23.30	22.10
1971-72	22.20	25.50	20.70	24.10	22.70
1972-73		not available			
1973-74	23.20	25.10	22.00	21.60	23.30
1974-75	23.30	23.70	22.80	22.70	23.40
1975-76	24.50	24.90	24.40	23.40	24.50
1976-79		not available			
1979-80	26.00	27.10	24.80	22.40	26.00
1980-81	27.20	28.20	27.30	21.90	27.20
1981-82	27.70	28.60	27.70	21.50	27.70

Source: U.G.C. Report for the year 1980-81 & 1981-82.

Table 2

Comparative Statistics of Percentage of Female Teachers in 1978 & 1986

	Different levels of Education	Percentage of female teachers 1978	1986
1.	Primary level	27.37	30.56
2.	Upper Primary	22.76	32.18
3.	Secondary stage	25.70	28.12
4.	Higher Secondary stage	20.85	29.33

on a comparative study of some **educational problems** reveals the shortage of women teachers in **India**. Great disparity is revealed in the fifties and sixties when the number of women teachers at different stages is compared with the corres-

Introduction

ponding number of men teachers. This indirectly reflects the lacunae in terms of women's education compared to that of men as well as the opportunities given to women to take up employment outside home. The growth of the number of women teachers has a high correlation with the growth in enrolment of girls schools and women's colleges. Girls schools and colleges are usually manned by women teachers.

There is uneven distribution of growth at different levels of education. The growth in the number of teachers at primary level has been phenomenal, though not all teachers teaching in higher primary classes are graduates. The number of women graduates in higher primary classes has increased about eight fold, but there is a decrease in percentage from 6.9% to 5.5%. This is due to the disproportionate increase in the total population. The numbers in vocational teaching and for higher and professional education do not show much growth, especially when these figures are compared with those for men teachers. The statistics show continuing disparity in the education of boys and girls. Thus in planning for the future, the country should give high priority not only to the expansion of women's education, but also recruiting many more women teachers at all levels of education in this development decade. The need is particularly urgent at the college and professional levels where the number of women teachers is pitifully small.

Although there is an improvement in the education of women after 70's, especially in terms of literacy level, education at the university level is challenged in its philosophy and programme. The conceptual thinking behind the educational goals is affected by the advancement of science and industry. The philosophical view has changed from an idealistic to a pragmatic view. The educational administrators will have to develop a professional eye and think in the context of the needs of the human capital that are required in constructing a very powerful educational system. Regardless of men or women, one should concentrate on an educational programme suitable for professional advancement and management capability. In the decades ahead, any organisation which ignores or underestimates the potential of women or overlooks any source of talent for that matter will be making a fatal mistake.

1.2 Women and Work

A common image of the work that women do is that of managing the home and children and the work that men do is to earn the family income. The statistics reveal that more than half the women who work for pay are married. This dual set of responsibilities results in a new style, tone and tempo of family life. When women work outside the home, a simultaneous change or adjustment has to take place within the role structure of the family members. The educational administrators have to take this into consideration while designing courses from the primary stage to the university level of education so that individual family is prepared to make adjustments to satisfy the competing demands and interests within their resources.

Today, women's contribution to the economy is not evenly spread. There is a strong tendency for women to be working at lower levels in industries and other occupations. In the west, women tend to be over represented in the clerical, sales, professional work in health and education, catering, hair dressing and personal services. Studies show that women are reasonably represented at the lower management level while they become dramatically under represented at higher levels of management. The reasons for the occupational segregation are:

(1) Conditioning of women in performing the same tasks/jobs.
(2) The orientation of the economic system to channel women into certain areas.
(3) Men's attitude and decisions channel women into certain areas.
(4) Women's education and training does not equip them

to work in certain areas, boys tend to do more science subjects while women do more of arts subjects.

1.3 Familial Role Constraints

Many studies in the west point out that women face problems both inside and outside the home because of lack of support/help in child care and home work. Day care facilities are far from adequate and when exist, these are very expensive for middle or lower class women to afford. In some cases, the women face additional problems in commuting long distances to work. Adding to it, there are no widespread easily available arrangements for paid house care.

A woman is likely to feel defensive about leaving her children. Our society still approves mostly of the mother who supervises and cares for her children. Although, these women have a dual role to play, they are often made to feel guilty for not remaining at home as full time mother.

The nuclear family which has emerged as a viable unit through industrialisation increase women's conflict between responsibilities at home and expectation involved in paid work. The cultural values and social structures women live with are based not only in classes and interest group but also in constraining sexual system. It is increasingly evident that the many limits on women's work exist within a broader system of patriarchy (Hartmann, 1981) in which women are kept subservient to men.

Considering the career stages and time perspectives, the late twenties and early thirties are very important for establishing oneself in a career. This stage corresponds to a women's strategic period of stress and constraints which she has to cope up. Unless sufficient support system is built up, it is very difficult to establish commitment to a career or institution at this stage. If a young person is successful in connecting with a situation in which one feels comfortable, the period of thirties and early forties is one of growth. For most successful people, this is the time of great sense of expansion.

1.4 Sex Discrimination

There are several sociological studies done both in India and abroad which showed that there is discrimination against women in terms of opportunities available to them. Owing to a general misconception about the ability and role of women in science and technology, there has been serious neglect in educating women in science. The studies also indicate salary differentials for men and women for the same rank of profession. The rate of advancement of women through the rank tended to be slower than that of men on an average. Most of the colleges have very low representation of women in administrative positions. The data from a survey of 265 major companies in United States reveal that 66% of them had been subject to sex discrimination. Numerous studies in United States emphasise on salary differentials between men and women in various disciplines, work settings, ranks and years of experience. Some studies also indicated that women faculty are evaluated on the basis of different criteria than males at the time of recruiting. Even a quick survey of the present status of women in academics reveals that the universities have not discharged their responsibility of eradicating discrimination at all levels. About 66% of the women employees on college and university faculties earn the same salary as that earned by 28% of the men in the same category. The actual number of men employed in all levels is 500% greater than the number of women. Beach (1985) in the case study of affirmative system in United States reported that women are under represented in Faculty and Administrative positions and decision making bodies. She also reported about the salary differentials and the decline in educational opportunities for women in the seventies.

One conventional argument is that industrialisation or modernisation leads to growing equality for women. But the Japanese experience does not reveal this. Women are virtually excluded from managerial or professional positions in Japan.

A conflict of allegiance exists for women with children who enter the work force but not for men with children. Through

Introduction

paid employment, men fulfil their family responsibilities while career and family life are presented as mutually exclusive alternatives for women. The irony is that women are allowed to work most readily in those jobs that provide the least flexibility to balance conflicting demands. Most women work at uninteresting jobs with rigid time schedules. In professions where there is flexibility in time use, women are poorly represented. The commitment required by this devotion is a primary allegiance that conflicts with the cultural mandate of women's primary responsibility to family.

Bourno and Wikler illustrate some of the problems women face in trying to combine professional and family life. They introduced the concept of the discriminatory environment. This idea indicates how current understanding about the meaning of commitment and sex restrict women from demonstrating their value and ability in non familial employment. On the other hand, women who have reached the top showed no difference in administrative ability.

Some studies on the comparison of the productivity of men and women faculty indicated that there is little difference between the sexes in terms of the number of publications as well as in professional experience, although the proportion of women to men faculty depicts a low figure.

Research carried out in the United States of America tends to draw the conclusion that women's abilities are seriously underrated in business. Women review ideas more thoroughly and size up work situations more realistically than men according to a survey carried out at De Paul University, Chicago.

Women's strong points include abstract visualisation, defined as the ability to work well with abstract ideas in which 75% of women excelled in tests as opposed to 50% of men. Women if transpired were good at working with numbers which leads one to believe that there should be more of them in areas such as accounting, auditing and statistics.

Another important point which is slowly being recognised is that when it comes to classic management skills like time and resource management, there can be few better training grounds than being an efficient housewife and organising a husband, a home and children.

1.5 Sex Differences

Although women and men are often debating about similarities and differences in the professional front, scientists have collected data on the characteristics on both the sexes for many years. They have concluded that there are some differences between them physically and psychologically. They state that men seem to be more confident than women mainly due to the physical characteristics like size, strength, vitality and also probably the most authoritative account of psychological differences. Boys are more socially oriented and more suggestible. Men have greater sense of control over their own fate and they may have more confidence on school related task. These reasons promote for the decisive nature inherent among men.

In essence, there are two causes for sex differences: genetic and environmental.

Genetic Differences

Human characteristics are transmitted from generation to generation by genes which are found in almost every cell of the body. The genes control the chemical reaction of the cell and the chemical reaction determines the cell's shape, size and function it performs. The cells make up the tissues and organs that make the human body. The genes are threaded together on strings called chromosomes. Chromosomes always act in pairs and there are 23 pairs in almost every cell in the human body. If a characteristic is located on one of these chromosomes, it cannot give rise to a genetic sex difference. However, there is a substantial sex difference in the 23rd chromosome. There are 2 varieties, the X chromosomes and the Y chromosomes. They are similar but in Y chromosomes one part is missing. In females, almost every cell has two X chromosomes. In males, every cell has one X chromosome

Introduction

and one Y chromosome. The genes carrying sex linked characteristics are located on the part of the X chromosomes which is missing from the Y chromosomes.

One of the sex linked characteristics in the production of male sex hormones is androgen. A person with XY chromosome will normally produce androgen. A person with XX chromosome will not produce androgen (usually they produce female hormones). Under normal circumstances, the production of androgen is under direct genetic control and in turn there is a clear and direct link between the levels of androgen and aggression. Men are found to be more aggressive, confident and decisive than women. The presence of androgen clearly affects the development of the gonads and muscular and skeletal tissues. It has also been suggested that at an early age, it can also affect the way that the brain is wired and this explanation has been given for the difference between the sexes in the spatial ability.

Environmental Causes

Another factor which makes a difference between male and female is due to the environmental causes. One explanation of many sex differences is that boys are taught to be male and girls are taught to be females. A society shares the behaviour of its members by rewarding approved behaviour and punishing unwanted behaviour. This process of teaching people to behave in expected ways is known as socialisation. The main agents of socialisation are the parents and siblings. Besides them, grand parents, friends and teachers are also important socialising agents. The socialisation pressure revealed a surprising degree of similarity in the rearing of boys and girls. Within the overall framework of equity, there are some differences which probably can be only explained genetically. Experience in the West shows that the parents treat a child in accordance with their knowledge of child's temperament, interest and abilities rather than the terms of sex role stereotypes.

An alternative environmental explanation uses the concept

of modelling. It suggests that at an early age, children develop a sexual identity. They know whether they are male or female and they can identify other people of their own sex. They then observe the trends of things their own sex do and they imitate the behaviour. Thus boys copy their fathers and girls copy their mothers.

What are often interpreated as sex differences in work behaviour (aspiration, concern for other coworkers, friendship, leadership etc.) may be more accurately explained as organisational behaviours. Studies show that those who are disadvantageously placed whether men or women, limit their aspirations and are less likely to be perceived as promotable, thus completing the vicious circle. According to Fonda(18) career advancement for women is affected by a commonly held belief that men are better leaders than women. She argued that the way subordinates respond to supervisors is partly based on how supervisors assess their own present power. Thus, those who have powers are more apt to be liked while those without power are more apt to be disliked. She stated that worker behaviour is attributed to hierarchical structures rather than gender or personality differences.

Many of the sex differences are irrelevant to the performance of most management work. Neither size nor strength have a strong relationship to management efficiency. In many circumstances, some sex differences such as aggression may be counter productive. But, confidence, assertiveness and decision making abilities need to be fostered and cultivated.

Both the genetic and environmental factors are responsible for the under representation of women in administrative positions. In India, there has been a marginal increase in the number of women entering in administrative jobs in education. The principle of Equal Opportunities and Equal Remuneration Act of 1976 seemed to point to a very optimistic future for women in administrative positions in the seventies. Even then, in the mid 80's there are still few women in the administrative positions and still few at the top level in India.

It has long become obvious that we are not utilising the

Introduction

capabilities of women in the various fields of occupation even in the sphere of education, especially in administrative positions. One of the reasons which was pointed out over and over again is the dual responsibility women hold which bring additional stresses on her compared to men. Consequent to the familial role, she is less mobile. They are kept in stereotyped jobs where the aptitudes, intelligence, education and skills are not fully plumbed leading to great economical waste.

1.6 Facilitating Factors

In spite of all these constraints, there are several environmental factors which facilitate women in entering management positions. Many organisations are willing to place females in management positions which encourage women to enter into more and more of such positions. More and more women are choosing to be highly qualified which lends itself to job orientation. Moreover, the society has accepted the working women in all spheres of work. It is no longer a stigma to come out of her household to be involved in work. With more useful curriculum, and due to less stereotyping of education and of jobs into male and female categories, women feel free to pursue studies far more appropriate to the career. Some of the social and economic changes which have taken place in the society, have become facilitating factors for women's access to advanced training and employment. One of the factors is the increased age for marriage by law. Women themselves prefer late marriage to be able to pursue a career which facilitate them in entering executive positions much early in life. The society has accepted the working women in all spheres of work.

The high cost of living has necessitated women to undertake jobs and compete with men to retain the jobs. Since people would aspire for higher standards by having more money and thereby be able to consume more and more goods and services, which is only possible if women are gainfully employed. The household technology has advanced due to the introduction of new appliances, products and life styles. Now, it is possible for women to reduce the time of household work, thereby have more time at her disposal for employment outside home.

1.7 Women in Managerial Positions

There is a prediction of the decline in the number of qualified male candidates for management positions as well as a decline in the male's desire to play management role. The increasing emphasis on equal right issues will result in organisations turning to relatively untapped source of managerial talent, i.e., women.

The recognition of women as viable candidates for management positions has been a slow process. Today, while few knowledgeable people would question the intellectual competence of women relative to men, many still question the emotional suitability of women for the management role. Women are being recruited and hired for management positions, but in many instances with reluctance and apprehension.

In principle, the objective of a management job is to use resources in an efficient and effective way to result in more value than the initial resource. Women are used to observing this principle in managing the home. The way the administrators ensure the efficient utilisation of resources can be summed up by routine work, problem solving and exploiting opportunities. A manager must be able to spot opportunities, decide what opportunities are likely to be profitable and devise plans to exploit the opportunities. The major activities according to classical management theorists are planning, organising, deciding, staffing, controlling, reporting and budgeting. But the new system focuses on dealing with people, dealing with information and making decisions.

There are many researches done to focus attention on job model, i.e., working conditions, opportunities and problems as the main sources of explanations for what people do at work and want from work. On the other hand, the gender model focuses on personal characteristics, family characteristics and an assumed 'family first' commitment in explaining men's attitude at work and job related attitudes and women's work attributes/aspirations. Whatever model an organisation believes in, the ethos of an organisation and especially the style and personalities of its top management is likely to have a major impact on the scope and pattern of the career development of their women employees. A very negative attitude will mean that no woman advance beyond a certain low level. What is frequently found in the context is lip service support for women's career development on the part of the senior administrators coupled with indifference to actually formulating and implementing action programmes.

Where the organisational climate is oriented towards the development of human resources and in general seeks to establish participatory attitudes, open relationships and readiness to change, there is a greater scope for women's career development. The institution could formulate definite action programmes along the lines of identification of problem and establishing responsibility and accountability and creating confidence in women.

First of all, we require statistical information regarding how women compare in the organisation with men in various levels of jobs, accomplishment, reasons for resignations, and how they fare in top management positions. A formal mechanism has to be developed by which potential can be identified, development plans established and promotional opportunities reviewed which would encourage women to think about their own interests and potentials. Then it is possible to investigate other possibilities and make an intelligent choice and finally can be considered for promotions or for openings on an equal basis with men.

There are several researches done on various factors like capability, career orientation, supervisory potential, life style, dependability, emotionality and deference regarding women. Some studies show that women are regarded as less capable than men because of biological and personal characteristics.

Some women themselves felt inadequate to hold supervisory role.

The perception of men regarding the women administrators need to be examined in terms of their own attitude towards women in the work place and to also acknowledge and develop their talents and capabilities, which will make them similar in behaviour expectation of each other and in their aspiration about the kind of life they want. Finally the woman herself is the blocking factor in the managerial bid to succeed. Women have been held back by their own preconceived notions of their roles in educational institutions. The women's family roles as daughters, wives or mothers reinforce not only dependent attitudes but also explain the ease with which they can take an organisational rejection and turn to domestic fulfilment instead. This creates very real stresses and pressures both psychological and physical. Psychological strain is created by the need to conform to socially induced images of feminity and to be the perfect wives, mothers and homemakers. This produces many conflicts and burdens of guilt, which inhibit career ambition and progress.

Often management is seen as a male role and this is a difficult aspect for women to cope with, since they are still primarily stereotyped into atleast a partially domestic or family roles.

Lack of confidence is one of the biggest inhibiting factors in women's career development. This really queues back to our process of cultural upbringing. In spite of the environmental constraints, some women choose to work for reasons of their own. They behave in ways that conform their selection for advancement and more with high and rising aspirations and motivations, while some others appear less motivated and perceive themselves as having inadequate skills.

It would be worthwhile to investigate the personal demographics which would be correlates of the job demographics for those women in light of the organisational characteristics and requirements. In fact by investigating the perception of both men and women who hold senior positions in education

Introduction 29

should reveal some of the issues relating to women's lack of representation in the management of education and to make recommendation for the development of appropriate in service management training for both women and men as the study would reveal.

The present study is undertaken with the following objectives:

1.8 Objectives
(1) To examine the perceptions of administrators in education in relation to the process of management particularly with regard to
   a. the demands made on them by the nature of their work;
   b. the constraints under which they operate;
   c. their perceived criteria for effective management; and
   d. the way in which they evaluate their own effectiveness.
(2) To identify the factors associated with the differences in the perceptions and managerial problems.
(3) To examine the implications of the results for further development of management courses in the education sector.

Chapter 2

Methodology

The initial research conducted was qualitative and exploratory in nature, which led to a series of structured questions with reference to the process of management. The final interview schedule was constructed in consultation with the co-ordinator from Department of Education Management, Sheffield City Polytechnic. Similar parameters were used as frame of reference for both the studies.

The interview schedule focussed on several aspects of management, personal and organisational background, goals and aspirations, stresses, constraints of resource availability, motives for working, the effects on the family, costs and benefits of working, administrative traits required, views on work opportunities and barriers to career prospects. An attitudinal survey on perception about women administrators was also included in the interview schedule. In an attempt to draw out more opinions than the questionnaire itself might elicit, space was provided for comments. Those comments yielded insights that numbers alone could not.

Two hundred administrators were contacted according to a list obtained from Bombay University and S.N.D.T. Women's University. Only those who were willing to participate in the study were interviewed. It required 2 to 3 visits to complete the interview schedule. The final sample consisted of 100 administrators, 35 men and 65 women administrators. [Table 3]

The sample consisted of comparatively more of men as senior administrators in relation to women. There were about the same proportion of middle level administrators in case of

Table 3

Profile of Responding Administrators

Characteristics	Administrators		
	Men(%)	Women(%)	Total(%)
Level of administrators			
Senior	22.86	6.15	12.00
Middle	71.43	73.85	73.00
Junior	5.71	20.00	15.00
Age			
<30	5.71	6.15	6.00
31 to 40	20.00	24.62	23.00
41 to 50	31.43	38.46	36.00
51 to 60	42.86	30.77	35.00
Years of experience			
0 to 15	8.57	7.69	8.00
6 to 10	14.29	15.38	15.00
11 to 15	17.14	16.92	17.00
16 and above	60.00	60.00	60.00
Formal education			
B.Sc./B.A./B.Com.	11.43	--	4.00
M.Sc./M.A./M.Com	14.29	21.54	19.00
M.Sc./B.Ed./M.A., L.L.B.	20.00	32.31	28.00
B.E./M.B.B.S.	8.57	--	3.00
Ph.D.	45.71	46.15	46.00
Marital status			
Single	8.57	26.15	20.00
Married	91.42	69.23	77.00
Divorced	--	4.62	8.00
Type of family			
Nuclear	65.71	76.92	73.00
Extended	34.29	23.07	27.00
Stage of family life cycle			
Beginning family	17.14	10.76	13.00

Family with Preschoolers	11.43	3.08	6.00
Family with Preschoolers and schoolers	8.57	4.62	6.00
Family with Schoolers	17.14	15.38	16.00
Family with Schoolers and collegers	28.57	27.69	28.00
Contracting family	8.57	7.69	8.00
Reasons for changing of job			
Better prospects	42.85	46.15	45.00
Promotion	49.57	23.07	32.00
Change of place	8.57	4.61	6.00
Married	--	26.15	17.00

men and women. There were more of women administrators at the junior level in comparison to men. In this regard the men and women administrators tended to have skewed distribution in the opposite directions. The women were concentrated in the middle and lower levels of management and they supervise fewer people (staff and students). Women are slightly younger in age group while men and women are equal in their educational attainments. About three-fourths of the sample were married. One fourth of the women were unmarried compared to less than 10% of the men. About 5% of the women were divorced.

Majority of the sample belonged to nuclear families, more so in the case of women administrators. The sample selected was strictly from the metropolitan areas and hence the sample presented such a profile which might be different in another town or rural areas. There was no difference in the proportion of sample belonging to the different stages of family life cycle, for men and women administrators.

Majority of the men and women administrators tended to have continuous work pattern profiles, although a higher percentage of women had a break in service due to marriage or change of place due to husband's job. More of the men administrators had promotions in their jobs compared to women administrators. Discussions were held with the

Methodology

administrators regarding the administration of the college/department. The comments made during the interview were written down after the interviewer left the room.

The responses were coded and analysed. Chi square and correlation coefficients were computed. The management effectiveness of the respondents was assessed by a five-point scale on various aspects and also by a self evaluation rating. Both the scores were correlated. The reliability of the scale was established by computing the correlation coefficient, which was found to be significant. The results of the study are discussed in the next chapter.

Chapter 3

Findings

3.1 Perception of Educational Administrators in Relation to the Process of Management

Management as a process is conceived differently by the professional managers and others. Some make things happen, the others watch things happen and the rest have no idea as to what is happening or what has happened. Almost all administrators feel that management mean getting things done. Administrative tasks have become the crux of management for administrators in education. Some feel that the process of management is a magic formula which can be used in all situations. This type of perceptions of solving problems by a formula reduces management to something which is passive or mechanical. The dominant trait of the manager who makes things happen is that he is goal oriented. It means further that he is actively and intelligently seeking that goal. The administrators of education were asked about their goal orientation. About 50% of the respondents were oriented to the goals of the organisation.

In educational administration, a lot of decisions are filtered from the top and also influenced by the governmental policies. Therefore, administrators have very little leeway in showing any innovative approach and accomplishing something unique. They have to invariably gear themselves to a standard and slow pace of achievement. But as far as personal goals are concerned, there was no apparent difference between women and men administrators. Among educational administrators, we do not find any strong commitment or motivation. Since

Findings

the targets are not spelt out in quantitative terms, there is no competitive spirit for achievement among individuals and among institutions.

When the aspect of task orientation is taken into consideration, about 50% of the sample were inclined to task orientation a great deal. The women were more eager to get work done than men in most situations. Men administrators seemed to be more business like in their work environment but women seemed to get around people a little more efficiently than men to accomplish the tasks.

Administrators follow different styles of management. Most of them felt that each one needs to be aware of the responsibilities they have and one needs to consult the superior in important decisions. About two-thirds of them felt that there should not be any directive management. However, some indicated that their subordinates were always diffident in making a decision and hence always wanted direction, which perhaps delayed the action in many situations. In one way, the second line of managers are not finding an environment for their personal growth and development and on the other hand, we face many situations where some of the administrative staff are not competent for doing the job and hence there is no scope for growth and development. In such situations, participative management becomes more and more difficult and as one of the administrators puts it, one is forced to resort to directive style.

In this study, the management process was perceived by men and women administrators somewhat similarly. Both felt that the management responsibilities revolved around getting work done, more so the men administrators. The academic administrators felt this was the only process of management in their programme. According to them, it is absolutely important because of the schedule of teaching work to be completed within a stipulated time.

The other responsibility which was mentioned by the respondents was organising programmes and maintaining liaison. More of the men administrators were oriented to this type of function. Academic administrators focussed on this type of activities and this was considered management according to them. Maintaining liaison, was another important function of educational administrators. Table 4 shows the priority of management functions of men and women administrators.

Table 4

Management Functions Perceived by the Men and Women Administrators

Functions	Men N	Men %	Women N	Women %	Total N	Total %
Getting work done	33	94.28	52	80.00	85	85.00
Organising programme	28	80.00	51	78.00	79	79.00
Maintaining liaison	25	71.42	43	66.00	68	68.00
Directing Research	5	14.28	2	4.44	7	7.00
Office Management	9	25.70	8	12.20	17	17.00

Management functions were perceived differently by different groups of educational administrators. Some identified the functions at a micro level while others identified the managerial functions at the macro level viewing the organisation as a whole. In this study the investigator felt that administrators did not follow any process of management while managing their organisation. There was no effort to visualise the future by determining how they would want the future to appear. Therefore, thinking about what one wants and how to accomplish it and determining in advance what is to be done is operationalised through the decisions one makes today. There was no evidence of planning of this nature for other things except budgeting of finances. It was also observed that when changes occur in the internal and external environment, consequent to that there was some management action required. Besides that, there was primarily a routine administration which was prevailing in many institutions.

Findings

Decision making was considered to be the prerogative of educational administrators and it has never trickled down the line of the organisation to promote the participative type of management. Nearly 50% of the administrators felt the need for involving the team in many decisions concerning the organisation or a programme. Surprisingly the others felt it was a waste of time to involve everyone in the process particularly because of the fear of indecision. Nearly 50% of them felt that a good manager should not be involved in making all decisions. Surprisingly more of the academicians felt that they should make all the decisions while the administrators did not favour this view.

The management style was observed in the institutions covered in the sample. The style followed in most of these institutions is directive style of management. Sixty per cent of the respondents agreed to this statement. They felt the subordinates did not have any initiative or self direction in reaching out for an organisational goal. The organisational growth is curtailed and people have become more and more dependent than independent. This throws light on the style which we need to promote in educational institutions especially with reference to the personnel selection and management. About 40% were totally oblivious of the evaluation at the administrative level. Interestingly enough, the rest of them were aware of the targets they wanted to achieve and what they have achieved so far.

Level of Direction

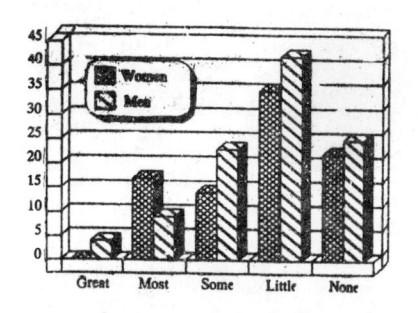

Fig. 1: Level of Direction in Management

Effective management demands a considerable knowledge of the disciplines that make up modern management, techniques for planning, organising, budgeting, controlling, staffing and the rest. Unlike business leadership, it does not necessarily require an extensive knowledge of the situation being managed. This conceptualisation is missing in the perceptions of these administrators.

Once the plans have emerged, the organisation with its power structure in mind would have to organise the management action through its people. This is achieved through delegation of responsibilities. One of the pitfalls in effective management is lack of delegation. Sometimes, the administrator does not enjoy the confidence of his team and hence wants to do everything himself which results in considerable delay in implementation. Other times, the responsibilities are delegated and people assigned for the same do not come to the level of expectation of the leader. The present study highlights the purposes of delegation as perceived by the administrator and how far the organisations are able to delegate the responsibilities.

The most important purpose of delegation as reported by the respondents was "to encourage a sense of involvement". Both the men and women administrators felt that this would surely bring about the participative type of management from all levels of the administration. The second important purpose as rated by men was to help develop skills and also training the subordinates.

The respondents in the study were asked whether they can delegate effectively in their respective organisation. All the respondents felt that they can delegate to a great extent. All the respondents were aware of the requirements for effective delegation. They have categorically stated that the requirements for effective delegation include

(1) Clear definition of tasks,
(2) Mutual trust,
(3) Adequate system of control,
(4) Subordinates ready to carry out decisions,
(5) Sound managerial judgement,
(6) Able subordinates,

Findings

(7) Working as a team, and
(8) Appropriate ratio between number of managers and number of subordinates.

Out of the eight characteristics spelt out by the respondents, working as a team was rated as the most important one. [Table 5] Whatever be the task, a team approach is essential for accomplishing the task successfully. The team members should be committed and in communication with one another to achieve organisational effectiveness. Unless they are morally involved and committed to the organisational goal, it is very difficult to develop a team approach and mutual trust. For this, one needs to be clear about the objectives or the goals. This is revealed from the responses of the administrators. They felt that the sense of identity is required by which they get the knowledge and insight into the organisation with reference to its goals and the management strategies it needs to develop. It is important to know to what extent the goals are understood and shared widely by the members of the organisation.

Table 5

Ranking by Men and Women Administrators on the "Requirements for Effective Delegation"

Factors	Men	Women	Total
Work as a team	1.5	1.0	1.0
Clear definition of tasks	1.5	2.0	2.0
Mutual trust	1.5	3.0	3.0
Able subordinates	3.0	5.0	4.5
Sound managerial judgement	4.0	4.0	4.5
Subordinates ready to carry out decisions	6.0	6.0	6.0
Adequate system of control	5.0	7.0	7.0
Proper staff strength	7.0	8.0	8.0

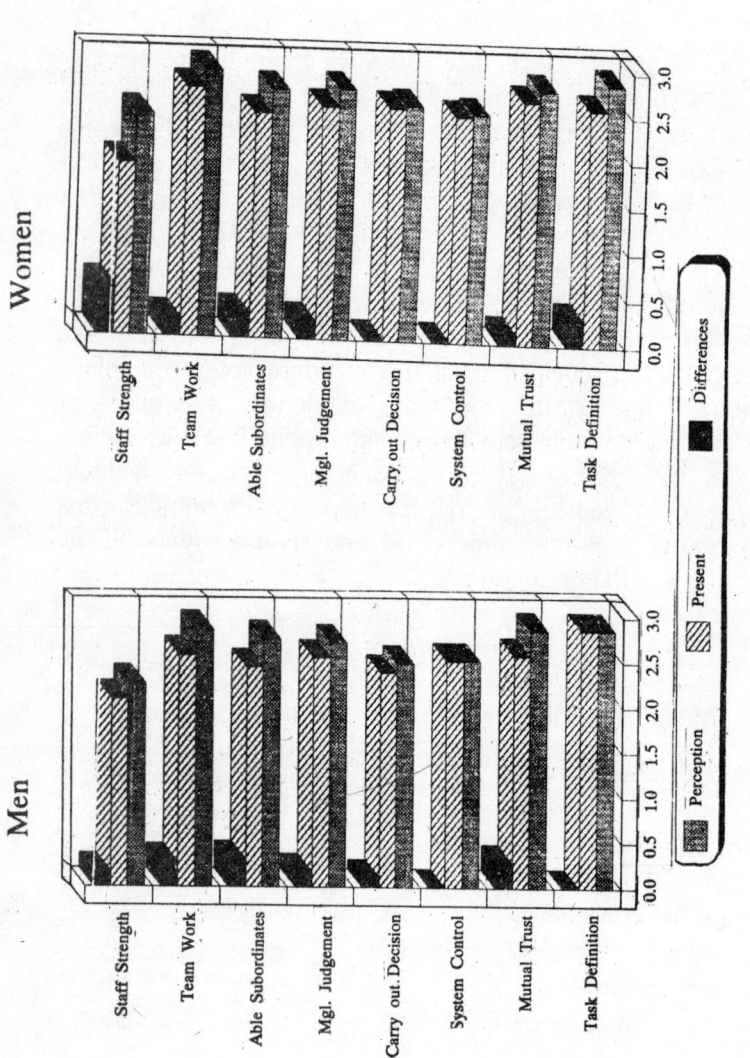

Fig. 2: Perceptions of the "requirement for delegation, the actual status" and differentials for men and women administrators

Findings

Supporting the three major requirements as discussed above, there are other factors like able subordinates and sound managerial judgement on the part of the leadership. Sometimes the financial constraints do not facilitate to attract the very capable persons to apply for an administrative job in education. Sometimes, the methods used for selection, testing and training of employees are likely to produce an image in the minds of the employees that the organistion is relatively indifferent to their personal needs and capacities. Sometimes employees learn early in their career to withhold involvement, make their performance routine rather than responding to demands for change. Sometimes you see the employees get thoroughly demoralised when there is no sound managerial judgement from the administrators. When the organisation gives this confidence of security and good judgement in terms of decision made for the organisation and its employees, people are willing to work together as a team to accomplish the organisational goals. Subordinates are ready to carry out decision in this context. In spite of all these, sufficient system of control is required while delegating responsibilities. This is the crux of management control and achieving organisational effectiveness. Adequate staff strength is also essential to carry out work effectively according to the stipulated plan.

Analysis of the responses elucidated [Fig 2 & 3] regarding the requirements for delegation and how far the organisational framework is meeting these requirements, it is found that although there was always a gap between

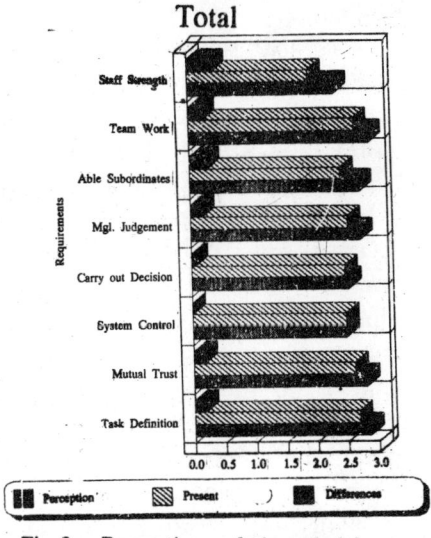

Fig. 3: Perceptions of the administrators regarding the requirements for delegation, actual status and differentials

the requirements and the status quo of the system framework and responsibilities perceived and carried out by the staff, wide gaps were seen primarily in terms of the objectives of the system and clarity of the objective among the members of the team. The expectations of the mutual trust and the ability of the subordinates and the team spirit and the present status in each of these factors also showed wide discrepancy. The most revealing discrepancy was found in the staff strength in the educational institutions required and actually possessed. These discrepancies clearly point out the need for management training in goal clarification, job responsibilities, interpersonal relationship and building up team.

Perception of men and women administrators were the same with regard to clear definition of task, adequate system of control and able subordinates and sound managerial judgement. Men considered mutual trust more important than women. Women specifically pointed out the need for having adequate staff. The requirement of working as a team was also emphasised by the women administrators more than the men. In the delegatory function, men did marginally better than the women.

It is also observed that there is a definite difference between institutions where management responsibilities are perceived to be routine work and the ones where organisational growth is given the focus. The latter was more effective in the management of education.

In the management process in education, one finds that because of lack of goal orientation, control stage of the management does not have a prominent place. Seldom the administrators pointed out that they had taken a review of the situation and made some modifications in the plans to achieve the intended objectives. Even in a crisis situation like teachers' strike, effective control of situation in terms of modified plan of action to reach the ultimate objective is not taken care of adequately. There is however a special need for checking and adjusting processes to be invovled in our academic and co-curricular activities — management to achieve

Findings

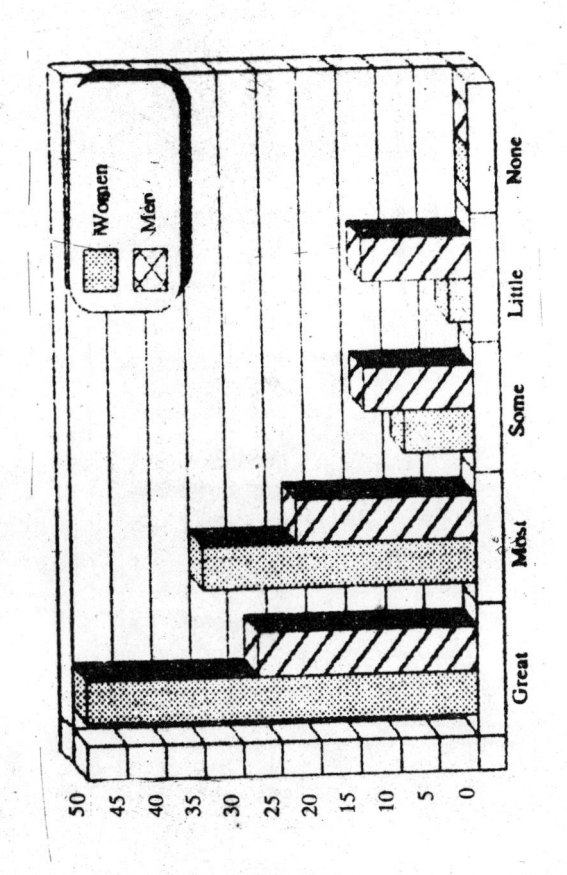

Fig. 4: Organisational goal orientation of administrators

Personal

Fig. 5: Personal goal orientation of administrators

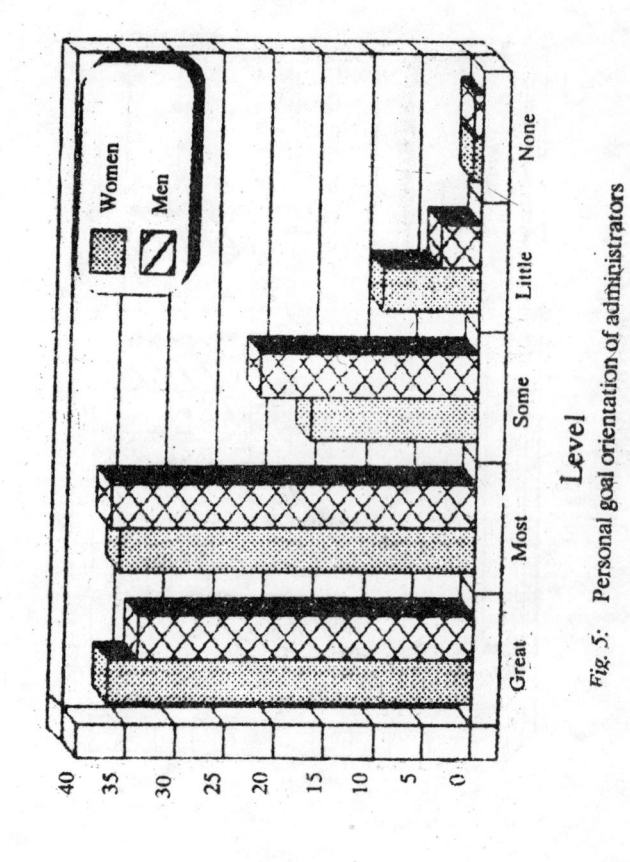

Findings

the optimum development of the students.

Evaluation is another process in the management which is not focussed in the educational administration. Evaluation in the educational administration only means the examination system. As far as the appraisals of the different personnel are concerned, not much importance is given although there is an efficiency bar to cross which somehow or the other is very leniently dealt with. Some of the administrators find that they have no time to review what they have done and accomplished. Most of the time they are busy getting things done and never review the situations. As a result, they do not have feedback to use it positively or negatively for further input into the management process in education and perception of the administration, a lacunae is felt right through in the process itself and even the absence of certain management processes. Certainly, when we review the educational administration, all these points have to be taken into consideration for management training.

In the managerial context, the men and women administrators were compared in the organisational goal orientation, personal goal orientation, task orientation and also the evaluation process of management. [Fig 4-6] All the administrators gave priority considerations to organisational goal orientation and task orientation. Women in both these areas scored more than the men showing the commitment to the cause she has undertaken. Personal goal orientation was the next item in order of priority where men scored higher than the women. With the traditional role expectations of men as the breadwinner, his personal goals and aspirations are higher than that of the women and hence this

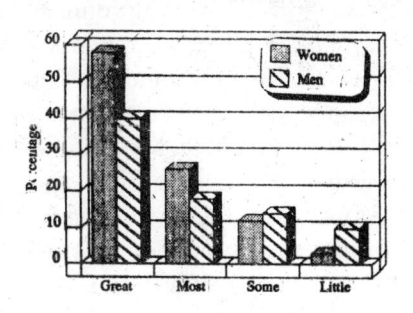

Fig. 6: Task orientation level of administrators

increase in score. Both the administrators follow a directive style of management and they feel that it is very essential to follow it since the subordinates are not ready for any other mode of operation.

3.2 Administrator's Time Management

An administrator's day is a sequence of responses to many situations. Some administrators respond to situations as they arise, another deal with the matters by defining the priorities. Some seem to be continuously coping with emergencies. Others live predictable and routine lives. Administrators at different levels show no significant differences in the time taken for routine activities. The time taken by the academic administrators is predictable compared to the administrators who did only administration. Those who have a combined function suffered in most cases, resulting in reduced effectiveness in the academic performance.

The most productive time is planned time dealing with priorities. The administrators in the study spent only a part of the time on planned activities. They seem to be always coping with emergencies and interruptions and most urgent matters thrust upon them from the external environment. Many of the adminsitrators stated that the planned activities have to be shelved in preference to the urgent demands placed on them by other systems around them. This highlights the need for all sub-systems working according to some predetermined plan and every one is well informed about the same.

The present study aimed to find out how the administrators divide their time for various managment functions. First of all the sample taken as a whole was not able to identify and separate out the time they spent for various managment functions. But they were able to give some framework according to the way they operated [Fig. 7].

In all management situations, decision making is an important facet of management because the decisions direct the actions. The process starts with the search for and identification of things to do and involves calculating the

Findings

Male

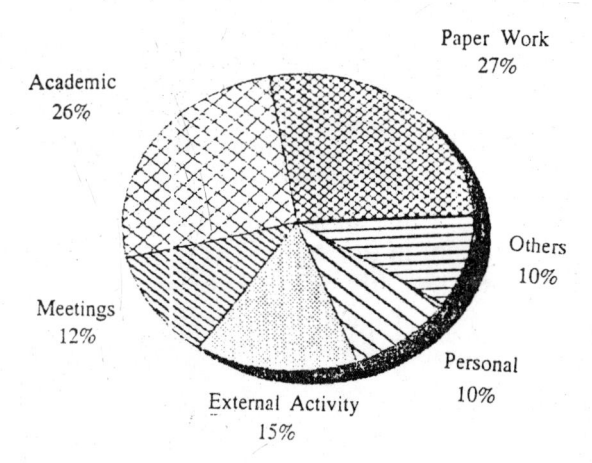

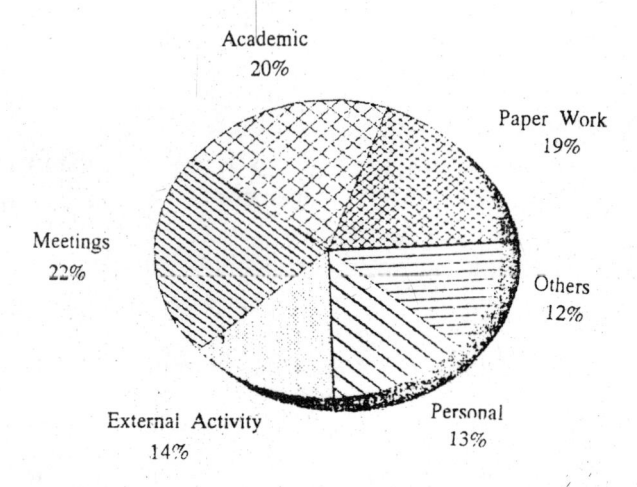

Female

Fig. 7: Time allocation for administrator tasks

consequences of each action. It ends with a commitment. In the present situation, the administrators were mainly concerned about the same decisions made in the academic councils, executive council, senate and other committees involved in academic as well as financial matters. Most of the administrators at the top level spend upto 50% of their time for decision making. But this constitutes only about 6% of the sample. Majority of the middle level administrators spend about 10 to 30% of their time on decision making functions. While those who are in the lower level of the administrative cadre spend less than 10% of their time on this function. Although the gravity of the decisions may differ, it is evident that all administrators take part in the decision making process.

Respondents on an average spent twice as much time in planning than in decision making. About 20% of them spent about 50% of the time in planning and 40% of them spent 15 to 30%, and the rest spent 5 to 15% on planning activities. Planning has been defined in many ways, but walking each activity through in advance of the action is one of the best ways to explain what planning is about.

In many situations of educational administration, it is noticed that many meetings are held for planning the course of action. But planning cannot be put into motion without defining who does what and who is accountable to whom. This is the organising function and this is not taken into consideration while specifying management responsibilities. In the absence of a well developed organisation and well understood structure, people move independently and more or less haphazardly. Administrators in the establishment section, heads of institutions, and supervisors spent some time on organising, and the rest did not respond to the time they spent on organising function.

In educational administration centralisation of power and decision making authority is the established norm. Although, administrators were aware of the function of delegation, some weaknesses in the process of delegation were apparent among educational administrators. There was an unwillingness to part with any significant segment of the work load. Majority of the administrators waste half of their time on details that could have been delegated. The other weakness was delegation of accountability without delegating the authority to carry out the assigned tasks. Therefore the administrators in this sample were unable to quantify the time they allocate for delegation.

Most of the administrators spent a considerable amount of time in getting things done. Implementing is an important management function they undertake. Greatest problems arise in this respect and that is the reason administrators spent a lot of time in getting things done, by telling people what to do and how to do it and keeping things moving. Apparently, they do not concentrate enough on their responsibilities.

Evaluating is another function administrators do not focus their attention except the top level administrators. They spent about 10% of their time for this purpose. Failure to audit the action has been the downfall of administrators in education. Unlike in industry, persons are not accountable in educational institution since each individual is not responsible for the growth of the institution academically or financially. When administrators audit the action, subordinates are motivated to do more because they know their contributions are recognised.

Controlling activities is done to some extent in educational administration but not enough to account for in terms of definite time allocation.

Opportunities to do new things can be found everywhere. But this happens only at the top level and hence at all levels of administration, the average time spent on this management function is negligible.

In general, about three-fourth of the time is taken up for administrative as well as academic activities. About one-half of the time is spent on doing as opposed to managing. Some administrators appear to be racing against the stop watch. Some do not take their full allotment of vacation days. All administrators start as doers. Those who display a willingness to do what they are told, and an ability to do things right are assigned increasing responsibility.

Today, administration often gets pressurised by many activities from trivial to major issues and problems. Men administrators spent more time on paper work than women administrators, while women tend to spend more time on other aspects connected with the organisation. When 72% of the men administrators spend more than 20% of their time on paper work, only 40% of the women spend the same proportion of time on paper work.

With reference to the time expenditure on meetings and external activities, both men and women administrators spend about the same amount of time. Twenty five per cent of them spend upto 20% of the time on meetings. About 60% of the men and women spend about 10% of the time on meetings.

Academics is one area where administrators spend their major part of the time since that is their main business compared to production in industries. Since the men do not have the additional responsibilities at home, they can afford to spend more time on this. Statisticians show that there are more number of eminent academicians among men compared to women. This probably is due to a number of factors interplaying on women, the constraints of time and energy because of the dual roles, constraints of mobility, the inability to make use of training facilities and the personality characteristics developed over the years which does not bring out the initiative for excellence.

Administrators spend their time differently. Twenty two per cent of the time cannot be accounted by women and 12% by men. Many administrators face some wasters from day to day, but some get succumbed to these pressures, while others have a better control of their environment. Some of the time wasters as mentioned by the respondents are visitors, commuting circulars, trivial matters, too many meetings, correspondence, conflicting goals, telephone calls, procrastination, unclear job description, preparing unnecessary reports etc. These interruptions take up a considerable portion of one's

Findings

daily work.

The time profile of the administrative section differs according to the level in the administrative cadre. The lower level administrators spend their time on procedures and processes. The primary skills in the middle management level cater towards interpersonal relations. To be effective at this level, one needs to influence people to work as a team member to build coalition and co-operation.

The top level administrator's concept of management is more of conceptual skills and ability to think strategically to perceive the whole picture, to understand how the parts of the organisation can be integrated. Of course, political skills and even technical skills to some extent are still important. Often these administrators feel that there is upward delegation while working towards organisational objectives.

The time management profile shows that the attitudes and beliefs in terms of time use need to have positive shift for both men and women administrators especially for women. They did not have realistic attitude about time use. The control of their time was dictated by external demands. The practice of open door policy and interruptions contributed to a great deal of wastage of time for both administrators especially for women. The academic administrators edged over administrators *per se* in their attitudes and beliefs about time use as well as their organisation pattern.

Many of the respondents gave equal importance to all the tasks rather than assigning priority to most important tasks. It was a pattern observed by all to finish the small tasks first and then to attend to the bigger tasks. Many a time, the bigger tasks always got left behind in the process. Some of them could not delegate the tasks effectively which resulted in getting work done entirely by themselves rather than getting it done.

The academic administrators were more effective in their time management mainly because they could demarcate the boundaries of their tasks more clearly than the other administrators.

3.3 Management Effectiveness

Management effectiveness in higher education is revealed in goal orientation, process of management, control, monitoring and evaluation. This would differ from institution to institution according to the leadership pattern, political and socio-economic environment, resource availability and student community. The effectiveness would include a mix of factors like setting realistic goals, having the aspiration and motivation to achieve the goals, managing one's resources taking carefully calculated moderate risks, ability to get work done by sound human relations, and long term vision of the future which could be acquired and developed. Tenacity, loyalty, strictness, simplifying ability, transforming individual performance into organisational performance, getting an experienced team to work with, conserving resources, resource augmentation and achieving academic excellence are part of the whole managerial profile of effectiveness. All these aspects are taken as a composite measure of effectiveness. The following table summarises the managerial profile of men and women administrators.

Table 6

Managerial Profile of Men and Women Administrators

Administrators	Effective	Somewhat	Ineffective	Total
Female	34 (52.31)	20 (30.77)	11 (16.92)	65
Male	12 (34.29)	10 (28.57)	13 (37.12)	35
Total	46	30	24	100

The data reveal that women by and large are more conscious about the management of their organisations. More than 50% of them were rated as effective compared to only 35% of men administrators. Surprisingly the percentage of administrators who were ineffective were more among men than women. The effective administrators attributed their success to the organisational climate and good planning, realistic goal orientation and full co-operation from the team. The reasons attributed to ineffectiveness are lack of co-operation, uncongenial climate, poor management, lack of planning and control and involvement of people. They also lack clarity of roles and often feel the lack of support from the management.

Management effectiveness is discussed in this study under the following heads:

1. Management effectiveness and socio-economic and personal environment.
2. Management effectiveness and the work environment.
3. Management effectiveness and the task itself.

Management Effectiveness and Socio-Economic Background

Management is planning and implementing a course of action which is only a throughput to the system approach where the managerial system is constantly interacting with the environment. There is always a demand on the system along with the resources although limited in nature provide a facilitating situation for management to take place. Along with the opportunities one perceives in the environment, one also confronts a limiting situation, i.e., the constraints. An administrator has to balance out both and make management as effective as possible within the political, economic and social constraints.

Whenever we discuss about women managers one tends to think in terms of different constraints they face in performing their job well. Women's role in the home is much more complex and involved than that of men especially with reference to the caring for the members of the family. One often tends to think that the extent to which women feel the constraints depend on the type of family she lives in. The present investigation reveals that those belonging to joint families tend to do the job more effectively than those who live in nuclear families. This is particularly true for women administrators because of the support they get from family in performing their familial role. The stress experienced by those who live in joint families is less than those who live in nuclear families due to the sharing of familial responsibilities. The mean effectiveness score for women was higher than that of men in both types of families. The women in joint families scored better than the women in the nuclear families obviously because of the familial support they receive from the relatives. When they are asked about the constraints and opportunities, they categorically mentioned the cultural and familial support they received to enable them to do the job well. This type of support might not be as forthcoming in the western family system as it is in India.

Fig. 8: Management of effectiveness and type of family

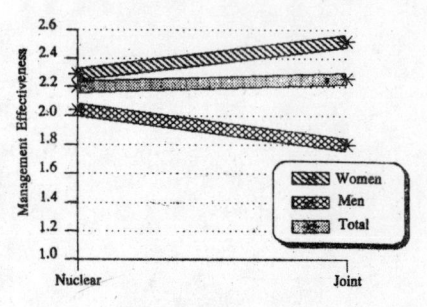

The expanding and school going stage of family cycle definitely show a decline in the effectiveness score for men and women administrators both in nuclear and joint families. (Fig 9) The beginning and the contracting stages show the highest score for management effectiveness. The women administrators belonging to joint families have a higher score in all stages including child bearing state. During the contracting stage, women in nuclear families also face family responsibilities like marriage of children, taking care of grand children and looking after old parents etc., even if they live separately. Joint families are a source of strength and support for the women when they go out for work. But for men, it takes a reverse trend. They tend to perform better in a nuclear family situation when they have to independently manage the financial burden of the household. In Indian households, usually men are not affected to that extent by the familial roles since these responsibilities are culturally

Findings

Family Life Cycle
1. Beginning family/single.
2. Expanding family.
3. Families with school going children.
4. Families with school-collage going children.
5. Contracting families.

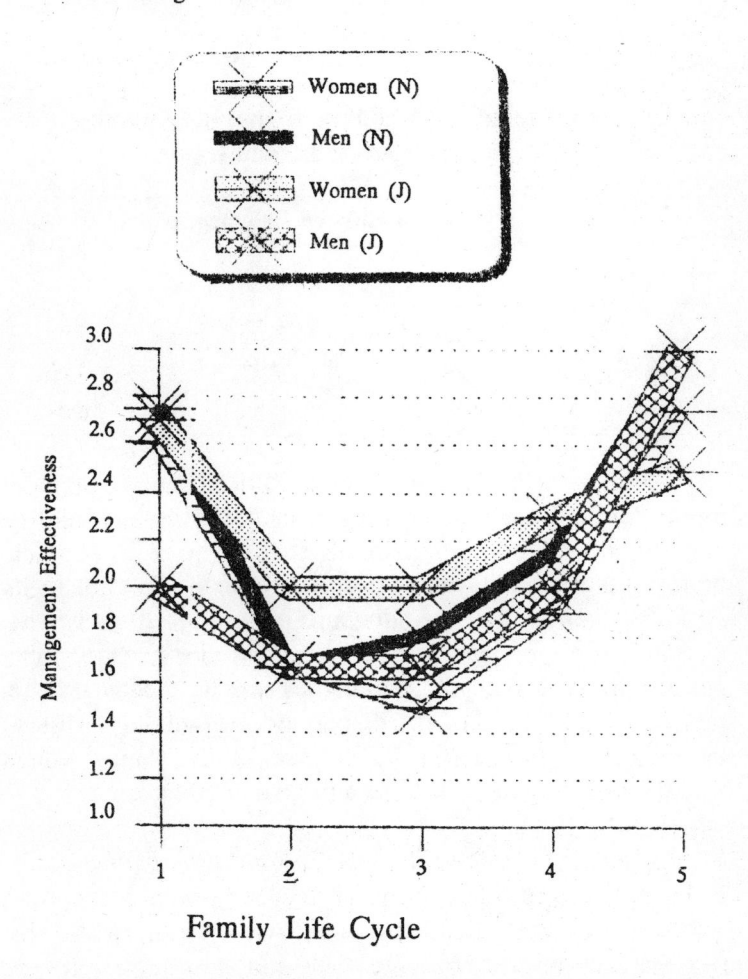

Fig. 9: Management effectiveness and family life cycle

assigned to women.

In the urban setup, one often finds constraints in getting domestic help to supplement the household labour. If proper assistance is received by the women, they are able to perform much better in their jobs. The following table illustrates the extent of domestic help available and the relative effectiveness in the job.

Table 7

Management Effectiveness and the Extent of Domestic Help Available for Female Administrators

Type of help	Management Effectiveness (%)		
	Not effective	Somewhat	Effective
No help	42.86	50.00	7.14
Part time help	13.64	22.73	63.63
Full time help	6.89	27.58	65.51

Regardless of the urbanisation and other changes happening in the family system, basically women are shouldering the responsibility of the home. All adjustments need to be made by her if she is employed outside the home. It is seen from Table (7) that as they get adequate help, their effectiveness increases to a great extent since they can devote more time and attention to the job. When they are torn between the household job and the office job, the household responsibilities get preference in the interest of the family which would apparently make her less effective on the job.

Management Effectiveness and the Personal Environment

The effectiveness in managerial job is determined to a great extent by the individual's aptitude, value system, aspirations, goal orientations and other personal characteristics. A few of these parameters have been investigated in relation to mana-

Findings

gement effectiveness.

The career motivations within an individual or the climate prevailing around him can affect the effectiveness on the job because this moulds his commitment to the task he undertakes. The respondents were asked about the factors determining the career decisions and motivations. Each one had a different set of reasons for undertaking the specific career. Table 8 illustrates the frequency distribution according to the different factors specified by them.

Table 8

Factors Determining Career Decisions

Factors	%
Ambition	55
Personal interest	38
Encouragement by parents	22
Determination	21
Suitable combination for career and family	7
Monetary benefits	6
Career counselling	5
Healthy competition	3
Scholarship	3

The most important factors determining the career decisions are ambition, personal interest, encouragement given by the parents and teachers and determination. More than 80% of those who possessed the characteristics of determination and personal interest were effective on the job. Personality and interest in the job have a remarkable influence on the performance of the job. The important factor was determination, for the male administrators. The reason attributed by women was encouragement by teachers and parents. The self awareness, self motivation and the identification of needs by themselves were lacking among the female administrators.

The structure of our society still demands that from early childhood, boys are brought up with the expectations to support themselves and their families. A girl's education still clings to the notion that she may only be marking time in a job and will have only herself to support till marriage. Sometimes girls drift into a job and become career minded. On the whole, she sees her job as evolving step by step rather than as a planned career with finite ultimate goal. Compared to that, men visualise a career as a progression, a path leading upward to recognition and reward. They would strive towards that goal by all means. The inbred attitude towards career development can be regarded as a built-in constraint created and maintained by women themselves and not by the environment alone. When women do not have the determination, they face a number of practical barriers which they are not willing to overcome. When the women are asked about the reason for change of job, they often attributed it to marriage and change of place. Only the few who are determined, would continue to strive for employment even after marriage.

The ordinal position was considered in relation to the effectiveness score and apparently there was not much relationship seen between the two variables.

Management Effectiveness and Education

Management as an art can be acquired or developed. Although management was specifically not taught in colleges and universities as a component in the curriculum, one acquires some of the management education through general courses in education and the rest from experience. The following table summarises findings related to management effectiveness and educational level.

The analysis shows that there is no significant difference in the effectiveness of management according to the educational level. Even in the category of graduates, some of the administrators are very effective. Some although possess high academic qualifications do not make good administrators since they

Table 9

Management Effectiveness and Education

	Management Effectiveness		
Educational Qualification	Ineffective %	Somewhat %	Effective %
Graduate	0.00	14.28	85.72
Post graduate	5.55	33.33	61.11
Doctoral	31.25	27.08	41.61

$\chi = 11.4$ $\chi = 12.592 (.05.4)$

lack the aptitude and interest in administration. Educational administrators need to be trained for the jobs they have to perform. Traditionally, they gain this experience over a period of time and not through a specialised inservice training programme. A training programme of this nature might prove valuable in developing effective administrators.

Management Effectiveness and Individual Orientation

The managerial performance is often related by the individual's personality and his orientation to life in general. These characteristics are moulded by the personal social environment one lives in. When a person had the facility of living in an open society and sensitive to other people's needs and aspirations, then the attitudes and values developed over a period of time reflect in the managerial performance. The present study reveals that the authoritarian administrators tend to be less effective since it does not yield a congenial atmosphere for growth. This curtails the participant's initiative and motivation for any course of action.

The study further shows that those who follow an authoritarian style of management often face with the task of directing the subordinates and the subordinates always look for directions. Unless the organisational climate is oriented

Table 10

Management Effectiveness and Individual Orientation

Orientation	Not effective	Somewhat	Effective
Liberal	12.50	25.50	62.50
Democratic	28.57	28.57	42.46
Authoritarian	38.89	44.44	16.67

towards the development of human resources and in general seeks to establish participatory attitudes and open relationships, managerial effectiveness is difficult to obtain.

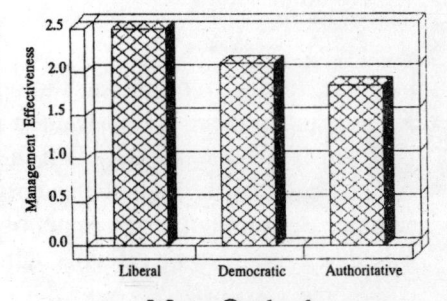

Fig. 10: Management effectiveness and management outlook

Managerial Effectiveness According to Marital Status

Among the sample, 77% of the administrators were married and 20% single and 3% divorced. Often management is seen as a male role and this is a difficult job for women to cope up, along with her traditional roles. Hypothetically, one would feel that a single woman is more like a man in terms of having no domestic responsibilities or other constraints related to familial roles. But some studies (Green galgh, 1980) show that career patterns of single woman are still more akin to those of other women than of men. Therefore this study probed into the relationship of managerial performance of men and women administrators with reference to their marital status. Table 11 shows the results.

Findings

Table 11

Management Effectiveness According to Marital Status

			\multicolumn{3}{c}{Management Effectiveness}	
Marital	Status	Mean	Not effective (%)	Somewhat (%)	Successful (%)	Total
Single	F	2.37	10.00	40.00	50.00	17
	M	2.00	33.33	33.33	33.33	3
Married	F	2.31	21.95	24.39	53.67	45
	M	1.93	36.67	33.33	30.00	32
Divorced	F	2.33	...	66.67	33.33	3
	M	-	...	-	-	-

The study shows that there is no significant difference in the managerial performance according to the marital status. There is a marginal increase in the effectiveness score for men and women administrators when they are single. There was no difference between the single and married women in the effective category. But in the ineffective category, the percentage for married women was almost twice that of the single women. Some of the married women seek employment because of financial reasons unlike the single women who always express their desire to work primarily because of professional interest and to be financially independent. This reflected in better commitment towards their profession.

Age also seems to be an important factor affecting the capacity of the administrator to increased input. The younger age group shows much more enthusiasm and would like to undertake the challenges in the administration unlike the older group who like to preserve and cherish the traditional approach to management.

Management Effectiveness and the Work Environment

Administrators often talk about the work environment in relation to the tasks to be accomplished and how effectively

Table 12

Management Effectiveness and Age

Age		Not effective (%)	Some what (%)	Effective (%)
Younger group	F	13.04	21.74	65.22
	M	55.55	11.11	33.33
Middle group	F	17.39	34.78	47.82
	M	38.46	46.15	15.38
Older group	F	13.76	41.17	47.05
	M	...	25.00	50.00

one can perform the task in congenial working environment. How this is accomplished depends on the organisation and its leadership.

Every organisation has a culture. It has its own cultural norms which dictate what are the expected and acceptable ways of behaving. These norms are mostly unwritten. They influence everyone's perception. Values also constitute part of the culture and it is an important component in the action scheme of individuals and which indicate the direction in which organisation is likely to move in the future.

The climate of the system reflects both the norms and values of the formal system and their re-interpretation in the informal system. Organisational climate rejects also the history of internal and external struggles, the types of people the organisation attracts, its work processes and physical layout, the modes of communication and the exercise of authority within the system. Just as a society has a cultural heritage, social organisations possess distinctive patterns of collective feelings and beliefs, passes along to new group members. Educational institutions show marked differences in climate and culture.

Findings

In spite of the obvious differences between the cultures of organisations performing essentially the same type of functions, it is not easy to specify the dimensions of such differences. Members are clear about the judgements they make but not about the basic standards or frames they employ in reaching a judgement. Therefore a frame of reference to assess the organisational climate was not formulated for direct questioning. The assessment of the general organisational climate was rated for their individual institution. The investigator's observation was also used to assess their status. Table 13 shows that more than 60% of the respondents reflected that the organisation to which they belong had a congenial climate. Only about 27% had mixed feelings about it and 12% felt that it was uncongenial.

The organisational climate was rated congenial when the respondents felt that they have the right leadership, able subordinates and a good team. The uncongenial climate was attributed to interference from authority or lack of encouragement from the superiors.

The management effectiveness was correlated with organisational climate for the administration. The correlation computed was .65 which was highly significant which re-emphasises the need for encouraging and fostering the building up of teams which will facilitate task performance. While emphasising on the need of a rational man, one also needs to meet affiliative needs by creating various social groups for him extrinsic to the immediate work organisation.

The most effective management occurs in a congenial organisational climate. An organisation which is built on the assumption and values of self actualising man is more likely to create a climate conducive to the emergence of psychologically meaningful groups because of the organisation's concern with the meaningfulness of work. Whether a group will work effectively on an organisational task and at the same time become psychologically satisfying to its members depends in part on group composition. For any effective work to occur, there must be a certain amount of consensus on

Table 13

Dominance in the Organisation and the Organisational Climate

Dominance in the Organisation	Sex	Uncongenial No.	%	Somewhat No.	%	Congenial No.	%	Total No.	%
Male Dominated	M	6	37.50	3	18.75	7	48.25	16	48.48
	F	1	5.88	5	29.41	11	64.71	17	51.52
	T	7	21.21	8	24.24	18	54.55	33	100.00
Female Dominated	M	4	28.57	4	28.57	6	42.85	14	25.45
	F	1	2.41	14	34.14	26	63.41	41	74.55
	T	5	9.09	18	32.72	32	58.18	55	100.00
No Domination	M	0	0.00	1	20.00	4	80.00	5	41.67
	F	0	0.00	0	0.00	7	100.00	7	58.33
	T	0	0.00	1	8.33	11	91.67	12	100.00
Total	M	10	28.57	8	22.85	17	48.51	35	35.00
	F	2	3.07	19	29.23	44	57.30	65	65.00
	T	12	12.00	27	27.00	61	61.00	100	100.00

M=Male; F=Female; T=Total.

basic values and a medium of communication. If personal backgrounds, values or status differentials prevent communication, the group cannot perform well.

The respondents were asked whether they were pressurised in educational administration to achieve the goals. The responses varied according to the type of organisation they worked. Although all organisations have some goals to achieve, some organisations set very ambitious goals for them to achieve in which cases, the demands placed on the administrators are high. In this study, there were 11% of the respon-

Table 14

Management Effectiveness and Organisational Climate

Organisational Climate	Little Effective No.	%	Somewhat No.	%	Effective No.	%	Total No.	%
Net congenial	11	91.60	1	8.33	0	0.00	12	12.00
Neutral	12	44.44	11	40.74	4	14.81	27	27.00
Congenial	1	1.64	18	29.51	42	68.85	61	61.00
Total	24		30		46		100	

dents who felt they were under tremendous work pressure while 50% of them did not feel any work pressure and the rest felt there was moderate amount of work pressure. There was not much difference between male and female respondents to the extent they are pressurised. But the senior administrators felt the pressure of work than the middle or lower level administrators. The academic administrators felt the pressure to some extent especially when they have to pursue some academic programme for their professional growth. In educational administration, the measure of achievement is qualitative unlike in industry where quantitative measure of profit is the indicator for growth. In academic institutions, certain syllabi are prescribed and certain code of practice in terms of work load and examination pattern are to be followed accordingly. More than that it fails to measure the effectiveness of the administration in terms of achievement of goal. Therefore, in educational administration, one comes across more of routine administration rather than situations of managing innovative programmes where strategic planning is called for. This is the reason why we find certain laxity in the performance of certain educational institutions and there is absolutely no work pressure.

Table 15

Frequency Distribution According to the Work Pressure Experienced by the Administrators

Administrators	\multicolumn{6}{c}{Pressurised to achieve goals}
	Not at all N	%	Some what N	%	To a great extent N	%
Female	32	49.23	25	38.46	8	12.30
Male	18	51.43	14	40.00	3	8.57
Total	50	50.00	39	39.00	11	11.00

Analysis of the data according to the dominance in the organisation shows that there is no distinct pattern identified for male and female dominated organisations. Both seem to follow the same pattern. In the female dominated institutions, there is marginal increase of work pressure felt than the male dominated organisations. Comparing the situations of academic administrators, and the other administrators of education, the academic administrators do not feel the pressure to the same extent as that of the latter and hence you find the women always preferring the academic jobs so that she can combine her dual roles effectively.

Management and the Organisational Climate

Organisational climate is sometimes influenced by the management a great deal depending on the interest they take in the institution, its academic programme and its overall growth. Some of the institutions covered in the sample are constituent departments of the university and some are affiliated to the university where the management differs from institution to institution. Some take a very authoritarian view on all administrative matters while others take a *laissez faire* attitude and some have a very positive developmental and democratic approach. These varying situations have their own

Findings

impact on the administrators and their managerial performance. In this study, it was found that only 9% of the sample felt that there was very little involvement on the part of the management. Thirtyfive per cent of them had shared their concern to some extent, while 50% had a very positive developmental approach towards the administrative ideas and concerns. Table 16 shows the distribution of the sample in these various categories and how the management effectiveness is related to the management support.

Table 16

Management Effectiveness and Management Support

Management Support	Not effective N	%	Somewhat N	%	Effective N	%	Total
Little	1	11.11	5	55.55	3	33.33	9
Fair	7	20.00	14	40.00	14	40.00	35
Strong	16	28.57	11	19.64	29	51.79	56
Total	24	24.00	30	30.00	46	46.00	100

$\chi^2 = 6.88$; $\chi^2 = 9.48(.05, 4)$

There is no conclusive evidence from this study that the management effectiveness increases with the support of the management. It is a strong facilitating factor but all the same the administrators per se have to mobilise and manage the situation effectively. Although the findings are not

Fig. 11: **Management effectiveness and subordinate boss relationship**

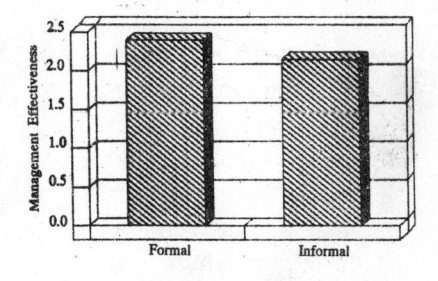

Table 17

Management Effectiveness and the Approach of the Administration

Approach	\multicolumn{6}{c}{Management Effectiveness}
	Not effective N	%	Somewhat N	%	Effective N	%
Formal	10	21.28	13	26.67	24	51.06
Informal	14	26.64	17	32.08	22	41.51
Total	24	24.00	30	30.00	46	46.00

$\chi^2 = 0.95$; $\chi^2 = 5.99\ (0.05, 2)$

statistically significant, there seems to be some trend in the increase in effectiveness according to the type of management support.

The management support also grows with the type of rapport the administrator has with the management. This arises out of the interaction with the management.

Table 17 shows the effectiveness in management according to the type of approach the administrators have with the management.

The Chi-square value does not show any significant result with reference to the type of approach and the management effectiveness. Table 17 shows that there is marginal increase in the effectiveness when the approach is formal.

Participative management is possible only

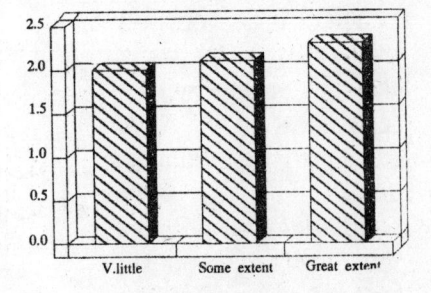

Fig. 12: Management effectiveness and the extent of interaction with the team

when the team member has the confidence to put forth idea to the administrator and the administrator responding to it in the most objective and constructive way. This is the challenge for human resource development. Some administrators resort to only directive management where there is one way communication. The present study reveals interesting results where some of them follow the participative management practices. When you consult and take collective decision, the group is bound by it and the collective efforts become the management input.

Table 18

Management Effectiveness and the Extent of Interaction with the Team

Interaction	Not effective N	Not effective %	Somewhat N	Somewhat %	Effective N	Effective %
Little	1	33.33	1	33.33	1	33.33
Some extent	9	28.12	11	38.38	12	37.50
Great extent	14	21.54	18	27.70	33	50.77
Total	24	24.00	30	30.00	46	46.00

$\chi^2 = 5.59;$ $\chi^2 = (0.05, 4) = 9.48$

Along with the participative approach, one should think in terms of the power and authority structures in the organisation to ensure effective leadership. Legitimate power in organisational life is an often discussed topic. The organisation has to co-ordinate and ensure the performance of people in different roles. Dependable role performance is made possible only if certain power is vested in the manager. Disorientation of power pattern in relation to responsibility is bound to have demoralising effect on all echelons of the organisation. The demoralisation encountered at the middle management level in many organisations is attributable in a large measure to a disregard for rational distribution of power amongst different levels of the organisation. Over a period of time, the responsibility pattern tends to conform itself to the power pattern. The whole managerial intiative is determined on this power pattern which should be consistent with the organisational goals.

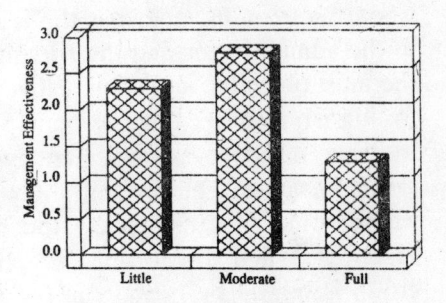

Power delegation
Fig. 13: Management effectiveness and power delegation

When the respondents in this study were asked about the extent of power vested in them, a great majority of them said that they had somewhat limited powers. Those who had enjoyed power to a great extent were effective in their managerial performance. [Fig. 14] The extent of power invested and the managerial effectiveness were correlated and it was found to be 0.59 which is highly significant.

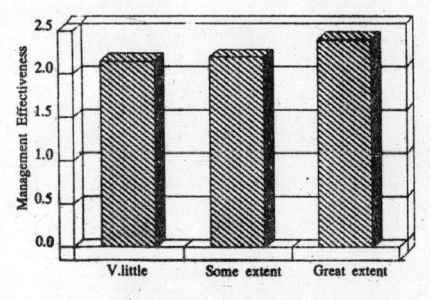

Power vasted
Fig. 14: Management effectiveness and power invested in the administrator

The study throws light on the fact that the administration has to be depoliticized and given more power and responsibility so that it can become truly effective. Autonomy within the administration would help speed up work. It should be revamped to make it result oriented. The respondents were of the opinion that the existing systems and procedures should be monitored to minimise or eliminate delays. Power along with accountability would make administration more effective.

Table 19

Management Effectiveness and the Power Invested in the Administrator

Power vested	Management Effectiveness					
	Not effective		Somewhat		Effective	
	N	%	N	%	N	%
Little	4	19.04	10	47.62	7	33.33
Somewhat	16	26.22	17	27.87	28	45.90
To a great extent	4	22.22	3	16.67	11	61.11
Total	24	24.00	30	30.00	46	46.00

Correlation r = 0.59; r(0.05,98) = 0.165

3.4 Administrative Tasks

Administrative tasks become the crux of management for administrators in education. How to accomplish the short term and long term goals of the organisation under the various constraints and pressures inherent in the system is a crucial issue for many administrators. Although the women administrators were not very vocal about the stress they were subjected to, through the questionnaire, they did mention a number of problems they experience stemming from stressors in the work, home, social and individual arenas.

The common high stressor for males and females were associated with lack of time, limited resources in terms of manpower and finance and increasing volume of work. Along with it, we often find the lack of involvement by the team in all the administrative activities.

About 20% of the respondents opined that there was no pressure inherent in their job. They were mainly academicians and they enjoyed working with the students and dealing with creative ideas and planning and implementation of the same.

Table 20

High Stressors for Female and Male Administrators

		Male	Female
1.	Lack of time	22.85	65.61
2.	Limited resources	37.14	27.69
3.	Increased volume of work	11.42	16.92
4.	Lack of involvement of staff	14.28	12.30
5.	Getting work done in spite of indifferent attitude	14.28	16.92
6.	Tasks not planned	8.57	10.76
7.	Absenteeism	22.85	18.46
8.	Inefficient subordinates	11.42	4.61
9.	Lack of discipline	5.71	6.15
10.	Lack of motivation	2.85	7.69

The benefits outweigh the costs and hence this group did not feel the stress in the process. The respondents who did not enjoy the administrative work mainly felt the stress more pronounced.

The home and social arena presented the stress situation for majority of the women because the managerial tasks of running the home was vested on them, while men expressed that they have no responsibility at home. The extra responsibilities a woman has to face all alone in the home front could be a deterrent in achieving organisational effectiveness. This study also reported similar findings. The women specifically mentioned about getting tired at the end of the day and also complained of too much pressure at work. This probably can be attributed to female biology and family responsibilities.

According to many of the respondents, administration and management were synonymous. They felt that some one who gets all the work done is a good administrator. It emphasises one fact that the crucial aspect of managing is not doing things

Findings

oneself but ensuring that things are done by other people. In principle, the objectives of management are quite simple, to use resources in an efficient and effective way so that the result is of more value than the initial resources. The way administrators/managers ensure the efficient utilisation of resources can be summed up under three headings: routine, problem solving and exploiting opportunities.

A manager must ensure that the day to day activities have to be running, for example, reports are to be completed, supplies are to be requisitioned and appropriate monitoring of staff and equipment is done from time to time. Relevant routine is vitally important and effective execution of routine is vitally important to managers, but there is more to management than just routine. Even when routine is effectively discharged, there will be time and circumstances when work is interrupted because of unforeseen events. Here the manager has the role of problem solving. Therefore the manager has to be alert in this respect of identifying the causes for the problem and what are the possible alternatives for solving the problem. Besides this, whenever opportunities are seen around, many administrators do not make use of them. The routine oriented administrator often gets into problems when it gets into a problematic situation or when some situations of change challenge them for effective management.

In educational administration, one finds many in the first category and very few in the last category. Therefore we find this setback in the effectiveness of management in education. In educational administration, one often comes across the situation of pleasant association with students in planning and implementing programme and promoting some creative ventures.

3.5 Work Profile

The work profile of an educational administrator consists of the management of academic component and the purely administrative tasks which support the system. The whole work profile of the administrative task depends on a number of factors, the strength of the institution in terms of the students, teaching and non teaching staff, the environmental factors and the initiative of the administrative and teaching staff to undertake new programme. The sample was assessed in terms of the management effectiveness and the task orientation. It was found that higher the level of task orientation, better the management score. (Fig. 15)

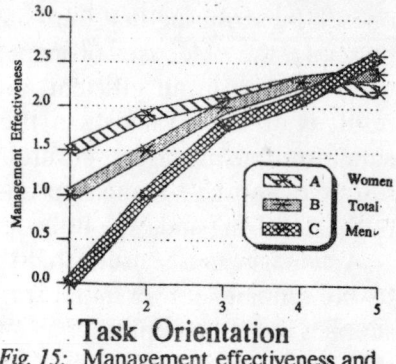

Fig. 15: Management effectiveness and task orientation

Among the sample, one third of the sample had student strengths of more than 1000 and about the same proportion had the strength of less than 400 students. Majority of them had a staff strength of less than 50 and the non teaching staff less than 10. Management effectiveness is higher in the smaller organisations. In relation to the strength of the students, the staff strength needs to increase proportionately and there should be a corresponding increase in the administrative staff strength. This is often mentioned by the staff as one of the constraints under which the organisations operate and they keep negotiating with the government for the same. In the actual situation, it was found that the effectiveness reduces and ineffectiveness increases with increased staff strength which only indicates that monitoring and control of the management functions should be based on optimum size of group so that all functions are done effectively.

Organisations have to be decentralised to the extent that they become viable units to operate as well as can be effectively administered. The optimum utilisation has to be taken into consideration for the staff as well as the physical facilities. The work profile of an organisation also depends on the number of programmes being offered and the number of staff working in the organisation.

Table 21

Management Effectiveness and Student Strength

Student Strength	Not Effective M	F	T	Somewhat M	F	T	Effective M	F	T
Small	38.46	7.69	17.95	30.76	38.46	35.85	30.76	53.85	46.15
Medium	25.00	12.50	16.67	37.50	31.25	33.33	37.50	56.25	50.00
Large	50.00	26.09	35.13	21.43	21.74	21.69	20.57	52.17	43.24

Besides the work at the office, an individual would have multiple roles to play in the organisation or in the domestic front, the tasks become more and more complex depending on the multiplicity of roles and responsibilities entrusted on the manager especially when delegation of responsibilities becomes difficult. Table 22 shows the additional roles and responsibilities of both types of administrators.

The additional responsibilities on the administrators whether male or female are more or less the same from the office front. Majority of the responsibilities stem from conducting seminars, workshops, guiding students and the research work. The additional responsibilities are undertaken by the administrators mainly to meet the organisational objectives and meet deadlines for accomplishing tasks.

If you look at the additional roles at home (Table 22) it was found that the respondents still carried out the main responsibilities in the home front. Majority of the home responsibilities are vested on the female administrators. Two-thirds of the men reported that they have no responsibilities at home. About 4% of the female respondents also stated that they have no responsibilities either because they get adequate help from the home front or they are not married. Many of the female administrators stated that some reallocations need to be done and articulate them properly to enable women to cope up with the dual role responsibilities.

Table 22

Additional Roles and Responsibilities of Administrators

Responsibilities	Male %	Female %	Total %
In the office			
Self development programme	11.42	7.69	9.00
Seminars and Workshops	14.28	18.46	17.00
Guiding students	14.28	16.92	16.00
Social work	17.14	6.14	10.00
Research	25.71	13.85	18.00
Extracurricular activities	8.57	10.77	10.00
At home			
No responsibilities	62.85	3.07	24.00
Management of family	31.42	60.00	50.00
Looking after sick and elderly	5.71	13.38	12.00
Looking after kids	5.71	18.46	14.00
Entertaining	0.00	7.69	5.00

3.6 Home and Social Arena

The responsibility of the home always is the prerogative of the women. As administrators although the man and the woman have the same responsibilities, when it comes to the home arena, the mother would take the major responsibility of ensuring a higher standard in upbringing children. The basic training a child receives from the mother is of paramount importance since growth is a direct result of improvement in the quality of child rearing.

The survey reveals that about 60% of the female administrators consider that managing the family is their responsibility while this responsibility is accepted by only one third of the male respondents. Looking after sick children is also considered to be the domain of the mothers and so as looking after elders and parents. Entertaining guests is not one of the popular area of work for educational administrators. This is done marginally by the women administrators. It was reported by more than 60% of the men administrators that they have no responsibility at home. They carve out an environment for themselves to be exclusively engaged in administative functions which facilitates better inputs.

3.7 Impact of Career on Marriage

Impact of career on marriage was positive as seen from the responses. Forty per cent of men and women administrators felt that it leads to a very positive assurance to both of them in terms of achievement and security. The women administrators particularly reported about their social development and feeling of fulfilling aspirations which enabled her to give quality input to the family services. Ten per cent of them appreciated the help they get from their spouse for fulfilling various functions which bring them closer. There is increased companionship between partners when they are involved in the administrative jobs. About one-third of the men responded that there is no impact of this career on their marriage compared to one fifth of the women administrators.

Table 23

Impact of Career on Marriage

Impact	Percentage of respondents		
	Men	Women	Total
1. Positive impact	42.84	40.00	41.00
2. Harmony	11.42	4.60	7.00
3. Fulfil aspiration	8.57	1.53	4.00
4. Social development	...	10.76	7.00
5. Shared experience	...	7.69	5.00
6. No impact	34.30	20.00	25.00

There were indications of some negative impact of marriage due to the administrative responsibilities. The significant factor reported was not having enough time for married life which was reported by few of the men and women administrators. Co-operation was lacking from the spouse in case of men administrators. There was a positive impact on children due to the educational career of parents. About 60% of them did not comment on any impact.

Table 24

Impact of Career on Children

Impact	Percentage of respondents	
	Men	Women
Educational impact	22.85	18.46
Childrens overall development & socialisation	17.14	20.00
Neutral	60.00	61.54
No time for children	20.00	3.07
Children's education neglected	2.85	6.15

3.8 Administrative Traits

Scientists have been collecting data on the characteristics of both sexes for many years. The review of existing research reveals difference, some based on unfounded beliefs and some on established facts. Some of the differences are physical and some are psychological. Men seem to be more confident than women mainly due to physical characteristics and probably due to some psychological differences (Maccoby and Jacklin, 38). Women are found to be influenced more by the socialisation process they have had from childhood and hence tend to be always assuming the familial roles as prescribed by the elders.

In the present study, the sample respondents ranked the men and women administrators on the following characteristics:

Confidence
Aggressiveness
Decisiveness
Competitiveness
Temperamental
Efficiency
Rationality
Sensitive to negative signal
Capacity for hard work
Honesty
Sincerity and
Creativity

Table 25 summarises the sex relatedness of important characteristics of administrators in education. Analysing the responses elucidated, it was found that there is an overall agreement between both the sexes on the characteristics of male and female administrators. The analysis shows that male administrators are more confident, decisive, competitive and aggressive than their female counterparts. The female administrators are honest, more efficient, sincere, confident and hard working. The common characteristic rated high by both men and women was 'Confidence'. Some of the cognitive aspects were rated marginally better for men and women were rated better in the relational aspects of working with people. There is no significant difference between male and female in the qualities required for an administrator.

Men administrators scored maximum on the characteristics of confidence. There is significant difference between the scores obtained for men and women, the score for women being lower than for men. This is one of the important characteristics required for any managerial position. Nearly 80% of the sample felt that the men are more confident compared to 56% of the sample feeling the same about women. Both men and women administrators agreed that the men are confident about their job while only 63% of women felt that they are confident. The perception of men regarding the confidence

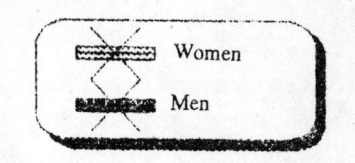

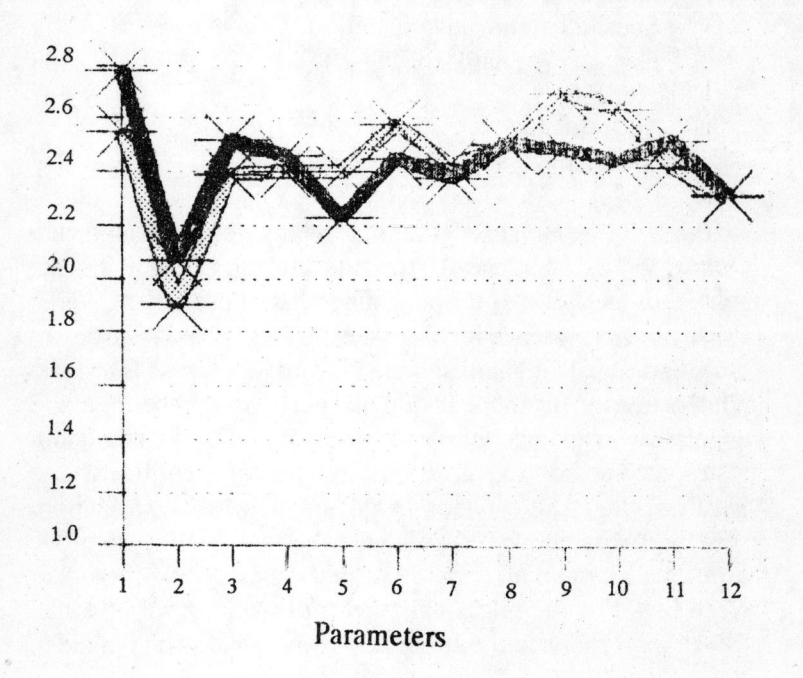

Fig. 16: Characteristics of men and women administrators on the following:

1. Confidence
2. Aggresiveness
3. Decisiveness
4. Competitiveness
5. Temperamental
6. Efficiency
7. Rationality
8. Sensitive to negative signal
9. Capacity for hardwork
10. Honesty
11. Sincerity
12. Creativity

Findings

Table 25

Sex Relatedness of Administative Characteristics by Men and Women Administrators

Characteristics		Rating Index			
		Women		Men	
Confidence	Women	2.63		2.79	
	Men	2.40	2.55	2.82	2.78
Aggressive	Women	1.86		1.98	
	Men	1.97	1.90	2.22	2.07
Decisive	Women	2.40		2.44	
	Men	2.37	2.39	2.65	2.52
Competitive	Women	2.45		2.47	
	Men	2.31	2.40	2.42	2.46
Temperamental	Women	2.18		2.12	
	Men	2.31	2.23	2.05	2.20
Efficient	Women	2.60		2.36	
	Men	2.54	2.58	2.60	2.45
Ratioral	Women	2.49		2.30	
	Men	2.31	2.43	2.51	2.38
Sensitive to negative signal	Women	2.33		2.40	
	Men	2.25	2.31	2.17	2.32
Hardworking	Women	2.41		2.40	
	Men	2.65	2.50	2.71	2.32
Honest	Women	2.71		2.38	
	Men	2.69	2.70	2.68	2.49
Sincere	Women	2.67		2.36	
	Men	2.57	2.64	2.60	2.48
Creative	Women	2.50		2.56	
	Men	2.25	2.42	2.42	2.52

level of women was very low. Only 42% of the men felt that they were confident resulting in a lower score for women on the whole. Sometimes, the social environment and the role script do not facilitate to develop this characteristic for women in our cultural context. However, it is encouraging to feel that more women feel confident of themselves contrary to the perception of men. In this competitive environment, it is essential that this trait should be cultivated more and more among women for their career development.

Aggressiveness was a characteristic rated low by many respondents. Men were considered more aggressive than women by all respondents. Men admitted that they are much more aggressive than their female counterparts. This trait is again a product of the hereditary characteristic as well as the environment in terms of the socialisation function. The respondents felt that in a competitive world, it is important to be successful and one can get work done only if one is aggressive at times.

Decisiveness is another characteristic for which men scored higher than women. Some studies indicate that women are slow in decision making and this is mainly because they consider all relational aspects which delay decision making process. When people are not that confident, they tend to live with indecision. The women respondents rated both men and women equal with reference to this characteristic, while men have rated themselves far superior to women in this regard.

Men are rated more competitive than women. There is not much difference between men and women's rating on men administrators. Although women feel they are competitive, men do not think so about women.

Women administrators are rated more temperamental than men in all research reviews. The present study does not show much difference in the rating for men and women by the total sample. Men scored women more temperamental than men while women considered both on more or less equal footing, with marginal increase in the score for women.

Efficiency is an important characteristic reiterated by management specialist. In this study, women are rated marginally better than men. The women considered themselves more efficient than men mainly because of the multiplicity of roles they have been thrust upon and efficiency with which they tackle them.

According to popular image and representation, women are considered to be less rational than men. In the present study, women are rated equal to men. When the women are trained for such administrative positions, one learns to be rational. Women consider themselves to be more rational than what the men rate the women to be. The women think they are more rational than men while men consider them to be more rational than women.

Both men and women administrators scored equal on the characteristic of being sensitive to negative singal. Once they reach a particular position they cannot be very sensitive to every issue that comes along.

Any organisation with some growth potential and orientation need to have a great input in terms of hard labour. Both men and women agree on this point and they are rated equally on this characteristic of hard work.

Honesty is an imporant characteristic highlighted for women administrators. Men rate both men and women equally on this score while women attribute a higher score for themselves compared to men.

Sincerity is another characteristic for which women scored more than men. Women rated themselves higher on the scale compared to men, while men considered both almost equal. Seventy per cent of the sample rated women to be sincere while only 47% of them rated men to be sincere.

Men scored marginally higher for the score on creativity, but there is no significant difference.

The participants were asked about the distinctive way they work as managers. Table 26 highlights the responses given by male and female administrators. The group as a whole agreed that getting the co operation of the team is the best way to be effective as a successful administrator. Male respondents had expressed this view more than the female respondents.

The women focus a little more on the team work and being considerate to people according to their needs within their

Table 26

Distinctive Way you Work as a Manager

Factors	Female N	%	Male N	%	Total %
Getting the co-operation	20	30.76	14	40.00	34.00
Good public relation	16	24.61	11	31.42	27.00
Self discipline	23	35.38	9	25.71	32.00
Team work	14	21.53	3	8.57	17.00
Making people indispensable	3	4.61	2	5.71	5.00
Quick decision	1	1.54	7	20.00	8.00
Proper planning and implementation	6	9.20	4	11.43	10.00
Hard work and sincerity	7	10.76	4	11.43	11.00
Considerate	12	18.46	3	8.57	15.00

own micro environment. Men have a wider perspective in public relations and getting the co-operation from all concerned agencies and the team work and also in making quick decision. Successful dealing with people is essential for effective administration. Communicative worker participation is possible in good team work where human relations are held in good esteem. A woman acquires this ability naturally in performing the familial roles. Realistic and attainable goals can be achieved by well defined objectives and subsequent planning and implementation. Men seem to be able to make quick decisions and plan and implement decisions better than women. Proper planning is essential for optimum utilisation of time. Besides planning, coordination of efforts is also required. The respondents were asked in this context to specify the characteristics of men and women which would be most appropriate for administrative positions. The following table summarises the data.

The responses from this study show two different domains

Findings

Table 27

Characteristics of Women according to Men and Women

Characteristics	Female N	%	Male N	%	Total N	%
Co-ordinating ability	17	26.15	12	34.28	29	29
Maintaining harmony	21	32.30	7	20.00	28	28
Patience	10	15.38	4	11.42	14	14
Hard working	26	40.00	13	37.14	39	39
Integrity	7	10.76	5	14.28	12	12
Balanced view	3	4.61	1	2.86	4	4
Greater sensitivity	9	13.85	0	0.00	9	9

of behaviour for men and women administrators. Men's views are more cognitive and conative in nature while women's characteristics are more in the affective domain of co-ordinating and maintaining harmony and performing tasks with earnest sincerity. In spite of the low rating in terms of cognitive ability and aggressiveness, women seem to be more

Table 28

Characteristics of Men according to Men and Women

Characteristics	Female N	%	Male N	%	Total N	%
Capable	5	13.97	6	17.14	11	11
Rational	23	35.38	8	22.86	31	31
Decisive	16	24.61	6	17.14	22	22
Practical	13	20.00	5	14.28	18	18
Less constraint	9	13.85	6	17.14	15	15
Daring	7	10.76	13	37.14	20	20
Mobility	2	3.08	1	2.86	3	3

effective in accomplishing the goals through the team work approach. Many respondents however pointed out that men and women do not have special characteristics attributable to the sex, but it varies from individual to individual depending on one's own attitudes, personality and initiative rather than the environmental constraints and opportunities.

In this study, the men and women were asked about the qualities required by an administrator in education. There were no significant differences between men and women in their views regarding the requirements. There were 3 clusters of qualities identified by both the administrators. The first cluster consisted of the top priority requirements, i.e., ability to deal with people and be clear about objectives. Women rated the quality of dealing with people as the top priority while men rated 'clear about objectives' as the top priority quality. Both are essential qualities, one for decision making and the other for implementing decisions.

The second cluster of qualities identified by the administrators are in terms of the effective qualities like being committed conscientious, communicative and having the quality of integrity. These qualities are essential for attaining the organisational objectives. The next set of qualities identified as qualities for an administrator are open minded, approachable, objective, able to lend an ear and ability to innovate. These were rated less important than the others. All the same, these qualities complement the previous cluster of qualities required by an administrator.

The last cluster of qualities identified as qualities required for an administrator are democratic, flexible, negotiating ability, able to accept criticism and warmth and sense of humour. The qualities rated least important by men were objectivity, democratic, flexibility, negotiating ability, warmth and sense of humour. According to women, only the last one of the qualities, warmth and sense of humour are not rated very high in the list of qualities required by an administrator.

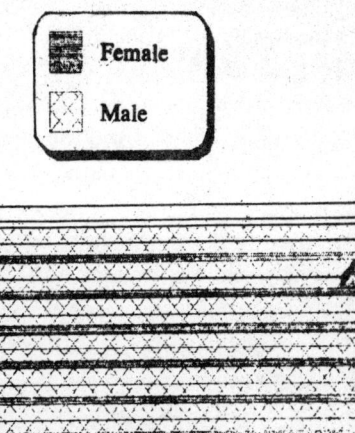

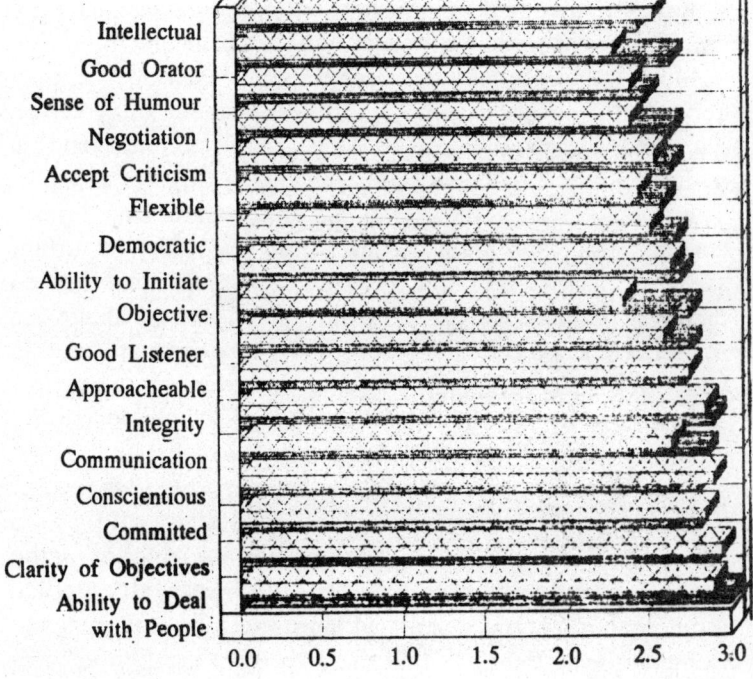

Findings

Fig. 17: Qualities required for an administrator

3.9 Perception about Women Administrators

In most societies of the world, women have been defined largely in terms of their functions as wives and mothers and by cultural image of their sexuality. Many people including women themselves think that they cannot think of performing any other role than wife and mother. Feminists tried to shatter this long held notion about women's place and the accepted belief of their nature and function. Even then, most women faced with the problem of dual role whenever they took up employment outside home. Despite the seeming progress, women still occupied inferior jobs and faced discrimination in entry to jobs as well as opportunities for advancement.

Most Indian women do accept their traditional role of dependence on male relatives. But as possibility of economic independence through respectable employment becomes a reality for women, they do take advantage of the opportunity. This study focuses on the perceptions about the female administrators and their family roles. The most important aspect of married female's employment is simply its effect on the level of wife's performance of family roles, including the household tasks. The data reveals that there is no articulation between female's and male's family roles. Majority of the men do not have any family responsibilities while the women are burdened with all the responsibilities. The educated Indian women in contact with a broader culture than that of her home learns about new role potentialities and would like to adopt certain changes in the traditional roles. In the background of this cultural context, the investigator studied the perception about women administrators by both men and women. The study shows that there are significant differences between the perceptions of men and women regarding women administrators.

In the 1980's, more than ever before, doors are opening for women. The present survey shows that the environment is becoming positively encouraging for women to take up administrative positions in educational institutions. The attitude towards women administrators by men and women was

Findings

assessed on a three-point scale with a number of attitudinal statements indicating the various issues regarding discrimination, representation, career for women, remuneration, employee morale and efficiency with women administrators, confidence and ability in leadership, competence, opportunities for women, their mobility etc. Figure 18 shows the overall picture of their attitude.

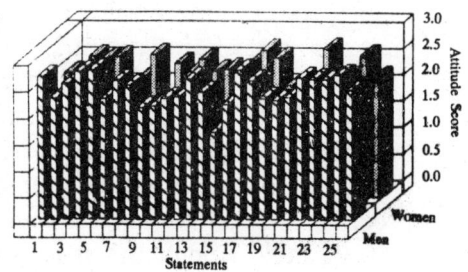

Fig. 18: Perception about women administrators

On the whole, women administrators are well thought of in our society. They have been scoring about 2.5 on a 3-point scale. Encouragingly the score given by men was more than that of the women. Therefore, with this attitudinal climate around them the future is bright if women are determined to make their profession a success.

Women and Discrimination

The respondents were asked about the issue of discrimination against women in educational administration. Perceptions about women administrators differ according to the men and women as seen from the responses elucidated from this study. Both perceive the situation differently. It reflects the experiences they had in the past and how they have related it

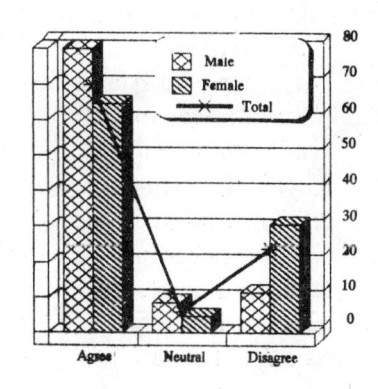

Fig. 19: There is no discrimination against women in educational administrator

to the organisational policies and the environment. Eighty per cent of the administrators feel that there is no discrimination against women in the field of education. However, a third of the sample women felt that they are discriminated against men. This discrimination is felt to a great extent in the male dominated institutions. In the organisations where there are predominantly more women or equal number of men and women, the discrimination is not felt to that extent. Sex wise difference in perception is apparent because the women are sensitised by certain stimuli from the environment and the men are mere spectators in the game.

Women's Representation

It has been pointed out over and over again about the under representation of women in administrative positions. The sample in the study were asked about their views about women's representation in educational administration. More than 50% of the respondents felt that they are well represented. In the female dominated institutions, the respondents felt that they are very well represented.

The enrolment of women in graduate and post graduate studies has risen to nearly 30% in the year 1981-82 according to the report of the University Grants Commission which indicates the increased potential for women to enter into professional job. But with only one third of the women having professional qualifications, it is likely that they are not equally represented in higher education or in administrative jobs.

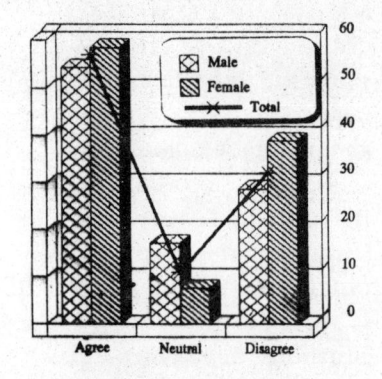

Fig. 20: Women are well represented in higher education

Educational Administration a Respectable Career

The representation of women in jobs vary according to the type of job and socio economic backgroud of the women. In the present study, the respondents were asked about their views on the educational career as a respectable career for women. Majority of the respondents felt that educational administration attracts able women because, it is a respectable career. People all over the world prescribed teaching as an ideal job for women. Even in educational administration, the job requirements and specifications do not pressurise them to that extent. Therefore, they are able to combine their familial functions without sacrificing on the family responsibilities of creating conflicts in their role performance.

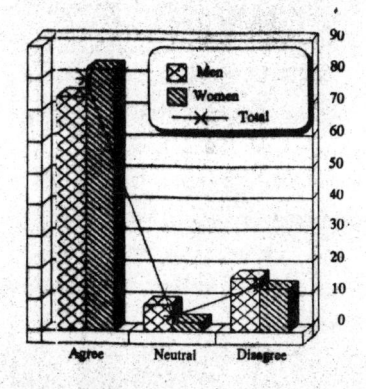

Fig. 21: Educational administrator attracts able women because it is a respectable career

Educational Administration Combines well with Familial Functions

Women prefer to take up educational jobs since it has some flexibility in terms of the demands placed on them, unlike some of the executive jobs which involve a lot of touring and heavy responsibilities. In this study,

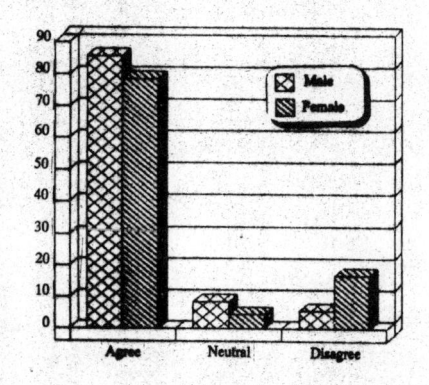

Fig. 22: Educational administration continues with marriage and family better than most careers

majority of the respondents felt that this particular career can easily be combined with marriage and family. In fact, 85% of the men compared to 73% of the women agreed to this statement. Almost 20% of the women felt that it was not that easy to combine both the roles unless there is equal support from the partner.

Educational Administration and Remuneration

Pay scales have been an often discussed topic among decision making bodies of the state as well as the central administration. Majority of the respondents felt that educational administrators are poorly paid compared to similar work in other profession. This was felt more strongly by men than women mainly because of the specific function expected of men in supporting the family. Generally, the income earned by the women is an additional income to the family. Therefore, there is likely to be some difference in the perception of men and women regarding the concept of adequate remuneration for the profession.

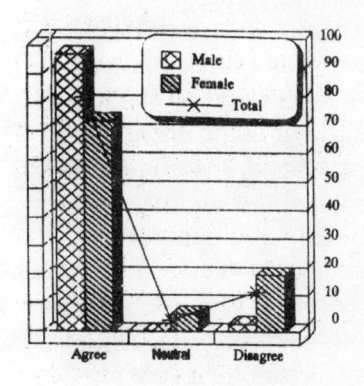

Fig. 23: Educational administration is poorly paid compared to other professions

Equal Pay for Men and Women Administrators

Generally it is felt that there is no discrimination in the pay scales for men and women administrators in education. The present study shows that over 85% of the men and 80% of the women felt that there is no discrimination in terms of pay for men and women. About 15% of women felt that there was some difference. Perhaps in some the privately owned

Findings

institutions, this type of discrimination is experienced.

Fig. 24: There is equal pay for men and women in the same educational administrative positions.

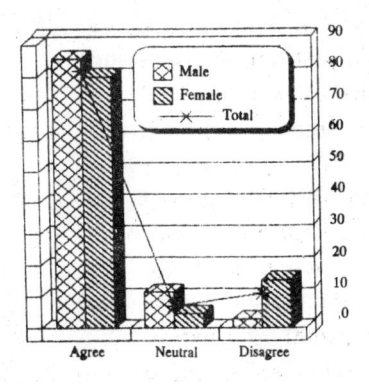

Men Working for Women Administrators

It has been the practice over the years that women work for men administrators and thereby assume a subservient position. When the situation is reverse, there may be certain amount of resentment among men. The present study shows a dichotomous situation in their attitude towards this issue. While 20% of the men in comparison to 50% of the women agreed to this statement, about half of the men compared to one third of the women disagreed to this statement. More of the women perceived that men dislike working for women administrators which may not be correct. However there is a difference in the perception of men and women with reference to the acceptability of women as bosses.

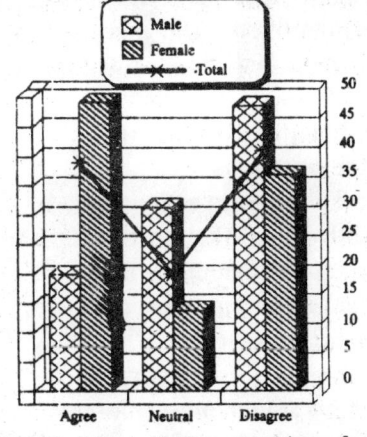

Fig. 25: Men dislike working for women administrators.

Women Working for Women

One would generally feel that women working for women is an ideal situation when both the subordinate and the boss understand each other and agree on a working formula for better coordination. When the administrators of the present study were asked whether in their opinion "women dislike working for women administrators or not", majority of them disagreed with this statement. Among those who agreed with this statement, women scored

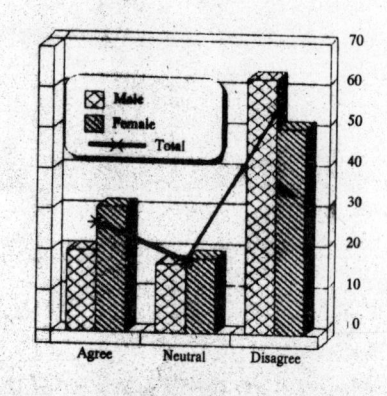

Fig. 26: Women dislike working for women administrators.

higher than men which indicates a 'strange phenomenon'. Over 60% of the men felt that women enjoy working for women. Only 50% of women think on similar lines.

Women Working for Men Administrators

The respondents in the study were asked to react to the statement "women dislike working for men administrators". There was strong disagreement to this statement by more than 60% of the respondents. Over 10% of the respondents agreed that women dislike working for men administrators.

Compared to the situa-

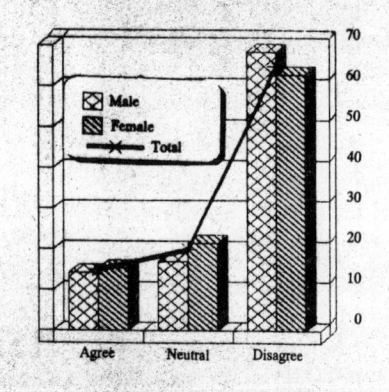

Fig. 27: Women disklike working for men administrators.

Findings

tion "men working for women administrators" and "women working for men administrators", the respondents are in greater favour for working for men administrator, given an option. Traditionally, women **are thought** of assuming a subordinate role in the family **and the same** is accepted in the professional setup as well.

Limited Number of Positions for Women

Although, generally people think that there are limited number of positions available to women for administrative jobs, the present study does not reveal the same view. While more than 50% of the women agree to this statement, 35% of the women disagree. The reverse was true for men respondents while 35% of them agreeing to the statement nearly 50% disagreed. There is a definite difference between the men and women respondents on this issue. Since many women do not get entry into jobs, they perceive the situation differently than men.

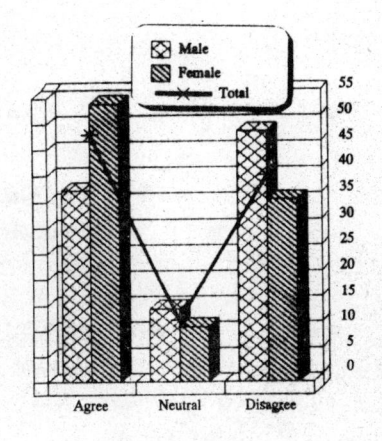

Fig. 28: A limited number of positions available to women for administrative jobs

Working Relations with Female Bosses

Accepting female bosses and establishing a working relationship with her is considered a new phenomenon. The present study reveals that one-third of the men administrators felt that it is difficult to keep good working relations with female bosses. Very few women felt the same way about female bosses. About 50% of the men and 70% of the women felt that there is no problem in working with female bosses. There were greater number of respondents (men and women) who disliked working for women administrators compared to men administrators.

Fig. 29: It is difficult to keep good working relationship with female bosses

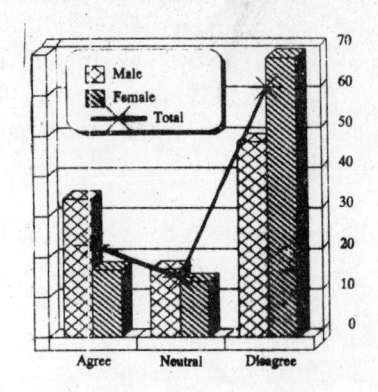

Perceived Effect of Women in Educational Administration

To determine how administrators rate women administrators' contribution in educational administration, questions were asked to the respondents to evaluate women's impact on employee morale and efficiency. More than 60% of the sample felt that the employee morale is least affected by having women administrator. However, over 30% of the men feel that the employee morale is affected compared to 20% of the female respondents. Some decades ago, men were not used to the idea of having women in the office situations. Since women always played a subordinate role in the home men used to feel that women will not be able to manage an administrator's job. But now the trend is changing. With the increased

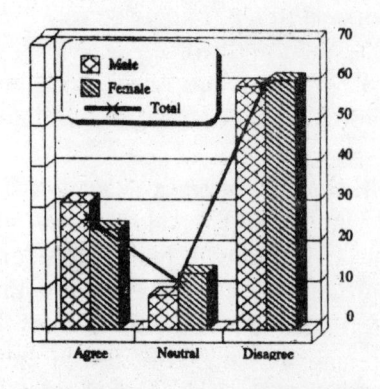

Fig. 30: The employee morale is affected to a great extent with women administrators

Findings

opportunities for education, women are getting more and more equipped to play this role.

Some studies indicated the lack of efficiency of women managers to cope with managerial jobs. Hence the respondents in this study were asked about their views on employee efficiency in the organisation with women administrators. About two-thirds of the respondents disagreed on this statement. This constituted 50% of the men administrators and 75% of women administrators. Men respondents were not very sure of the efficiency in the system with women administrators while women feel that there would be increased efficiency in the system with women administrators.

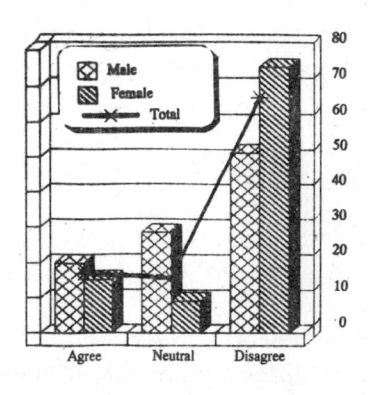

Fig. 31: Employee efficiency is affected to a great extent with women administrators

Women and Aspiration for Authoritative Position

People generally feel that women do not aspire for position of authority; due to the priority given to the familial role and may be because of lack of training to cope with various responsibilities. To assess the views of the respondents on this issue, the administrators were asked to react to the

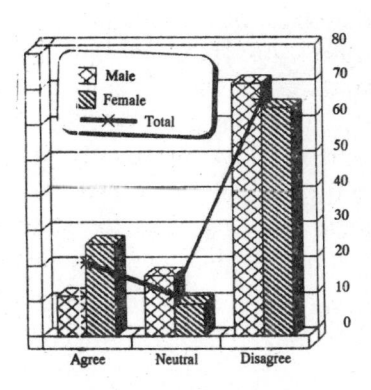

Fig. 32: Women rarely expect or want position of authority

statement "Women rarely expect or want a position of authority". Two-thirds of the respondents disagreed with this statement. More men disagreed to this statement than women. Both men and women feel that due to the advancement in the educational level and professional orientation, women are also equipped with necessary skills and traits necessary for managerial jobs. Women still lack adequate training for administrative jobs. Besides the training, the support from the home front and the organisational climate has to be congenial to enable women to undertake such responsible positions.

Women Lack Confidence

People in the past particularly resisted the idea of having women managers, since they felt that they lack confidence compared to men. The respondents in this study were asked to react to the statement "Women generally lack the (confidence) skills and training needed for a manager's job". More than 60% of the administrators disagreed to this statement. When 25% of the men agreed about women lacking confidence, 25% of the women also agreed to the statement. The data reveal certain amount of diffidence on the part of the men and women regarding the skills to be acquired by women administrators to assume administrative positions.

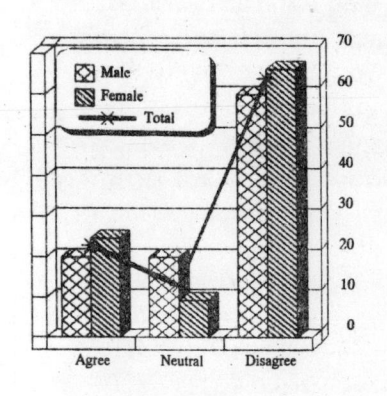

Fig. 33: Women generally lack the (confidence) skills and training needed for a manager's job

Exceptionally Good Women Succeed as Administrators

Since the tradition is the accepted direction of action,

Findings

generally women make a mark in their profession only if they are exceptionally good. Then only women and men give the necessary recognition to women managers. The situation is different for men since they are traditionally socialised to assume the responsibility of supporting the family financially through the investment of their human capital in the economy and receiving the necessary financial remunerations. This is the reason why 60% of the respondents opined that women have to be exceptionally good to succeed as women administrators. More than 35% of women do not agree to this proposition.

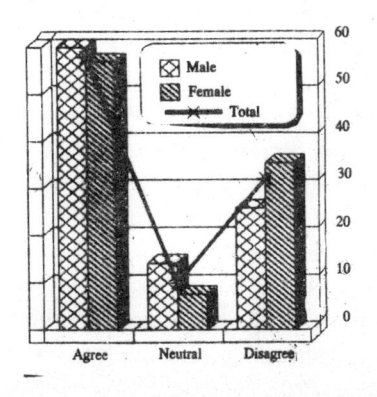

Fig. 34: Women have to be exceptionally good to succeed as good administrators

Women Want to Make Contribution to Society

Women of today want to make a contribution to the organisation by assuming powers of authority. They are confident of playing the dual role effectively. Some men expressed doubts regarding the motivation and commitment for professional goals. About two-thirds of the sample agreed to this statement. Almost 75% would want to make a contribution to society

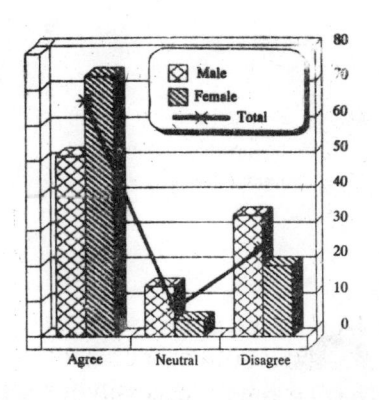

Fig. 35: Women of today want to make a contribution to the organisation through position of authority

while only 50% of the male feel the need for it. Women on the whole feel that they need to achieve some feeling of self fulfilment rather than be confined to only the domestic roles.

Women and Equality in Leadership

It was encouraging to note that women and men both feel that women administrators have the ability in achieving equality in leadership. About 10% of the respondents felt that they lack the ability in achieving equality in leadership. A large number of reports in the dailies and periodicals highlighted the subtle discouragement to women aspirants for positions of authority built in our system in spite of the Equal Opportunity Act. There is apparently a basic double standard latent in our educational system. A feminine perspective should exist parallel to the dominant male role and it must be integrated into all our systems if women are to be involved in the growth and progress of the country. Just like in the case of men, women also need to have the necessary input for human resource development which a particular job demands.

Fig. 36: Women lack ability in achieving equality in leadership

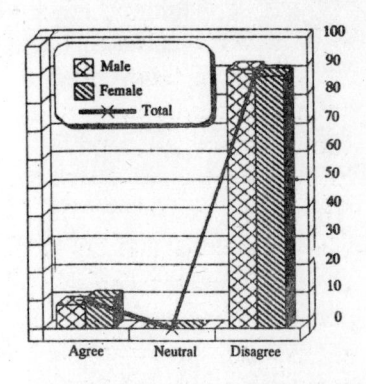

Work, a Necessity for Women

About 80% of the sample, both men and women feel that it has become a necessity for women to work since the cost of living has risen to a great extent especially in urban areas.

Findings

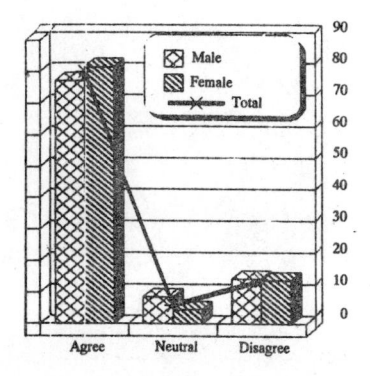

Fig. 37: Working has become a necessity in women's life

Women and the Dual Role

In order to assess the view of the respondents on the role women have to play, they were asked to react to a statement "Women cannot be thought of in any other role than wife and mother by many people". The responses elicited from the respondents indicate that about 50% of the administrators still feel that women cannot be thought of in any other role than wife and mother. It is encouraging to note that more and more men in this cultural setting have started accepting the role of women in other capacities than wife and mother. Surprisingly more women feel that they cannot be thought of in any other role than wife and mother. But women should work towards fulfilling this long cherished aspirations of professional advancement rather than a dependent attitude and the resultant role she assumes thereafter.

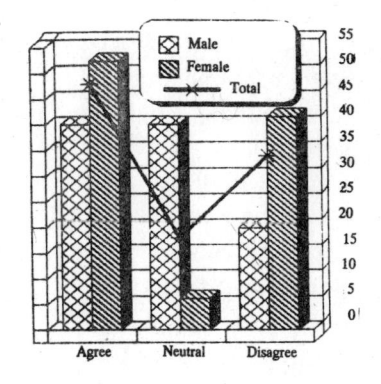

Fig. 38: Women cannot be thought of in any other role than wife and mother by many people

Women and Mobility

Women are less mobile geographically because of her traditionally accepted roles in the family. If the husband is transferred, the wife is expected to move along with him. In this study, 60% of the men felt that women are free to move if need arises.

The study pointed out that on the whole, women do not have an equal chance to succeed as administrators because of the constraints placed around her by the environment. Majority of the respondents felt that men and women should follow the same career path provided they have equal capabilities. In spite of all these orientations, majority of the respondents felt that women find less opportunities for advancement in educational institution.

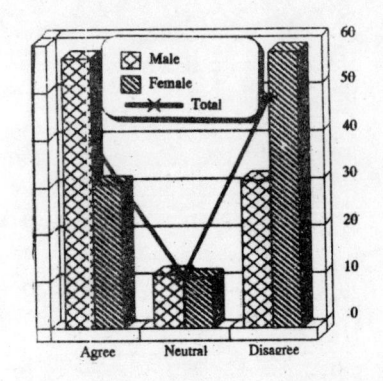

Fig. 39: Women do not have the opportunity for mobility if need arises

Women and Her Constraints to Succeed in Administration

Over 50% of the respondents disagreed with this statement. All the same 35% of the women agreed to this statement compared to 15% of the men administrators. Some of the respondents who disagreed might have support from the family to assume administrative position.

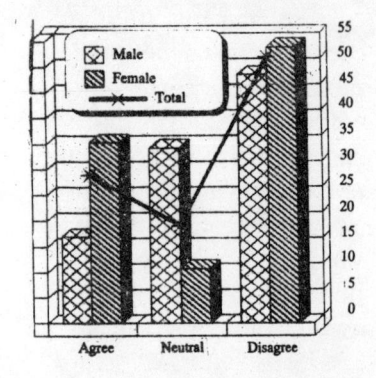

Fig. 40: Women do not have an equal chance to succeed as administrators because of the constraints placed on her at home

Findings

Women and Her Contribution

In spite of the double standards existing in the minds of the people relating to the employment of women, they all agree on one aspect of the environmental demands on the family from the financial point of view. The respondents in this study also stressed the importance of the women contributing to the family income due to the increasing cost of living. More than 80% of the sample asserted this point of view since this could create independence as far as their work and living is concerned financially and socially. Besides this, it would be personally satisfying for women to work outside home to satisfy her self actualisation needs. It would be gratifying for women to use her knowledge and skill to the maximum advantage.

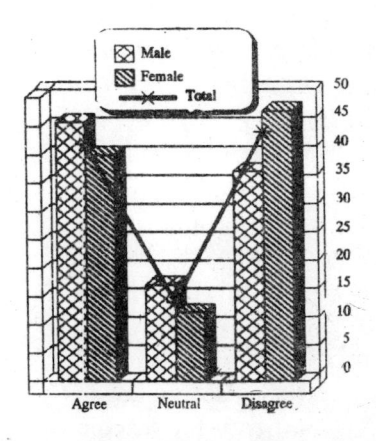

Fig. 41: Women do not have an equal chance to succeed as administrators because of the constraints placed around her by the environment by virtue of her age

Women and Career Path

The responses reveal that 87.7% female and 80.0% male respondents agreed to women having equal opportunity for career advancement. The female respondents are **more** strong in their view

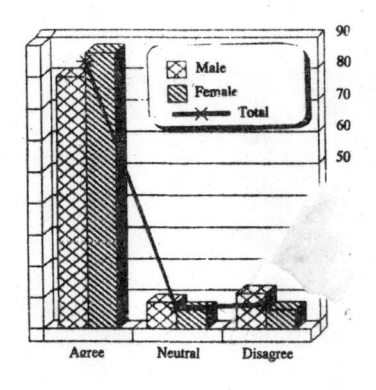

Fig. 42: Men and women should follows the same career paths if their capabilities are equal

regarding the equal opportunity for career selection and advancement.

Women Find Less Opportunities for Advancement in Educational Institutions

The responses elicited from the respondents indicate that about 80% males and 61% females agreed to this. A number of men felt that the women find less opportunities for advancement.

Majority of the respondents (81.5% females and 80.0% male) disagreed to this statement. That means the trend is towards positive involvement of women in administrative positions.

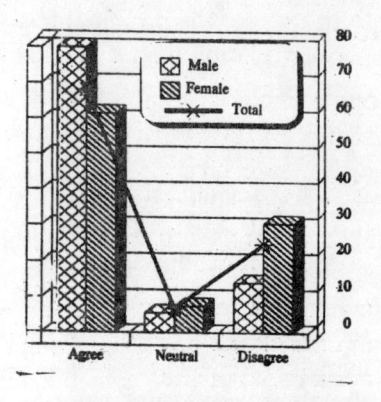

Fig. 43: Women find less opportunities for advancement in educational institutions

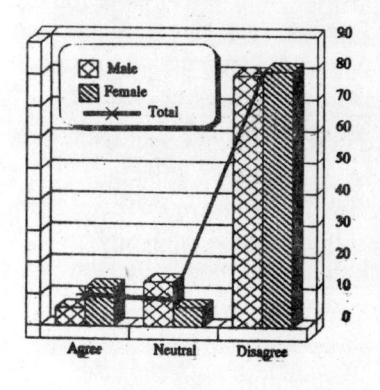

Fig. 44: Women are socialised to convey out household duties and therefore would be incompetent in administrative positions

3.10 Problems of Administrators

Women administrators felt certain stress in their job situations like tenseness, difficulty in coping with home responsibilities especially with reference to relatives. They felt that they are unable to influence and persuade people. Some times they felt that they are unable to cope well in conflicting

Findings

situations. There were cases of poor performance on the part of lower level administrators, both men and women.

Men administrators complained of not having enough opportunities for advancement. The task liked least by men administrators are paper work, monitoring, report writing, supervision, and dealing with peons and meeting with the union. Procedure constraints and non co-operation and absenteeism among staff are other aspects disliked by the men administrators. The female administrators also disliked paperwork, routine work and report writing. They also faced the problem of procedure constraints, supervision of personnel, non co-operative attitude of junior staff.

By and large working day for both women and men administrators rarely exceeded seven hours. Sometimes men had to continue working till late hours of the evening while the women attended to unaccomplished task in the morning. Very senior women administrators carried work home after office hours since the volume of the work is too much to cope with during the day with many interruptions about meeting and visitors. The role related stress arises from difficulty in allocating sufficient time and energy to conflicting roles. Three employment aspects, namely, satisfaction with the job in general, physical strains experienced and personal life satisfaction were examined in the present study.

The findings indicated that a large percentage of the respondents both men (65.71) and women (62.91) who had to assume demanding management roles experienced problems of role overload and inefffective role implementation to the extent that they expressed regret at being unable to devote time to academic and research work. One-sixth of the sample of women administrators found it difficult to cope up with the several daily interruptions in their work. On the whole, there was no indication of dissatisfaction with the job per se/or personal life or any physical strain.

Administrative tasks in education are not liked by many people because they feel compared to the inputs one does not get the satisfaction one deserves. While in case of academic

Table 29

Effects of Role Stress Associated with Administrative Tasks

		Percentage of response	
		Men	Women
1.	Job satisfaction:		
	(a) Unable to devote time to academic/research work	65.71	62.92
	(b) Difficulty in coping up with interruptions at work	8.57	15.55
2.	Physical strain:		
	(a) Periodic Tension	5.71	13.33
3.	Personal life satisfaction:		
	(a) Insufficient time available for family and social role fulfilment	5.71	15.55

activities one finds some personal satisfaction. While administrative tasks are very involving, it exposes the administrators, to the varied external systems and people. One also derives certain amount of status in the society, financial independence and opportunity for showing one's talents and also to certain extent self realisation.

Considering the extent of time use, administrative positions have certain disadvantages also. One is not able to do substantial amount of academic/research work. They keep having the periodic tensions and are unable to work without interruption and the most important sacrifice they make is, not having enough time for family and relations.

The constraints expressed by the men and women administrators vary in number and frequency. Women seem to be facing a number of different types of constraints than men. Men felt constraints in terms of government rules and policies and then financial constraints, while women felt more constraints deriving from the family and cultural role scripts and

Findings

also the financial and politicial constraints. To some extent, they felt the government rules and policies constraining their actions.

Promotions in the respective organisations are decided on merit, seniority and by virtue of professional contribution. Less than 10% of men and women feel that it is decided by virtue of sex. About 77% men and 67% women expressed that promotions are decided on merit. Sixty seven per cent women compared to 57% of the men mentioned that it is based on seniority. About one-third of the men and women felt that promotions are made on the basis of professional contribution.

Both the types of respondents were asked regarding the difference if any in terms of role performance by men and women administrators. Both agree that there is a difference in the role performance when the women and men assume responsibility. At the same time, majority expressed that there is no difference in the capability between men and women. But among those who felt there are differences, the following reasons are attributed for the same.

Table 30

Reasons for the Difference in Role Performance by Women

Reasons	Percentage of respondents	
	Men	Women
Women well prepared	11.42	16.92
Sensitive/considerate	31.42	27.69
Enforce greater discipline	8.57	1.53
Less time for women	5.71	3.07
Less mobility for women	8.57	3.07
Performance: Varies from individual to individual	33.27	15.38

It is generally agreed by men and women that women give more importance to the family, especially during the early years of married life which is seen from the different stages of family life cycle.

Table 31

Constraints

Constraints	Percentage of response	
	Men	Women
1. Government policies (political)	48.57	53.84
2. Financial	22.86	36.92
3. Temporal	2.85	15.38
4. Formalities/Red tapism	14.29	3.07
5. Family roles	...	49.23
6. Cultural constraints	...	53.84
7. Intellectual constraints	...	3.07
8. Emotional constraints	...	4.61
9. Unable to set career targets	...	6.15
10. Lower status in the male dominated society	...	9.23
11. Less opportunities	..	4.61

The present administrators reacted to the extent of aspirations they have in their mind for boys and girls. The male administrators felt that professional education should be given to the boys and they did not emphasise to the same extent for girls, although the picture is changing these days. All the same, they all wanted them to be good educated citizens. They wanted to leave it to them to decide their career. The female administrators on the other hand had no difference in their aspirations for their sons and daughters. Having gone through the dual career and experienced the advantages, they were of the opinion that their daughters also should have equal opportunities like their sons. The trend in socialisation of boys and girls of the present day is apparent from the findings of this study.

Findings

When the respondents were asked about their job expectations, majority of them felt that job satisfaction is very important. This was expressed by both, although there were more of the men administrators responding to the same compared to women. Women were more analytical about the cost benefit aspects of the job they undertake.

Chapter 4

Conclusions

Education of women is regarded as a key element in their quest for equality. The impact of education on women themselves, their family and society cannot be overemphasised. The contribution the women can make towards economic development of families and the economic system need to be monetarily assessed to see how much is lost if they are not involved in productive labour. Education and training alone can narrow the difference in competency and achieving empowerment of women and their social position and placement of the talent where it can be most productive.

The National Policy on Education emphasises promotion of women's education in all areas of learning to eliminate any sex based stereotyping. With the acceptance of gender equality in the Constitution, the plan of action should be simple. However, in the implementation stage, many obstacles creep in which directly or indirectly affect women's participation in education and in occupation.

The effective implementation would result if the individuals concerned have the necessary motivation and determination to pursue the education and the career, whether it is men/women. The immediate family and the social system should support the women's venture. The organisation concerned has to extend a helping hand to the women in actually formulating and implementing action programmes.

Where the organisational climate is oriented towards the development of human resources and in general seeks to establish participatory attitudes, open relationships and readi-

Conclusions

ness to change, there is greater scope for women's career development. The institution could formulate definite action programmes along the lines of identification of problems and establishing responsibility and accountability and creating confidence in women. If the organisation supports behaviour appropriate for organisational attainment, the result would be an effective organisation. In addition, the organisational culture may operate and enhance human values like giving an opportunity to make a meaningful contribution to the organisation, accept responsibility and also to have opportunities for recognition and advancement.

If the organisations are to develop a healthy climate, focus must be on both the formal system including goals, technology, structure, policy and procedures, the resources and the informal system including perception, attitudes, feelings, values and informal interactions. People in the organisation develop a psychological contract between themselves and the organisation. Work in the organisation becomes more enjoyable and meaningful, if feelings and sentiments are permitted to be a more legitimate part of the organisational culture. The team spirit within the organisation can contribute towards morales, productivity and human satisfaction. Therefore organisation development and team building are important aspects of management development in an organisation. These can be achieved if there is a common goal to achieve for the organisation as a whole through participatory decision making and management.

Besides the organisation culture, communication plays a major role in determining how effectively people work together and co-ordinate their efforts to achieve objectives. Employees work more effectively and with greater satisfaction when they understand not only their own job objectives but also those of their own work group and the total organisation. Besides giving the appropriate information to the group, communication should also play a great role in inter personal dynamics and it has its bearing on decision making process too. Decision making should be a process in which many persons in the organisation exert influences, besides, those at the policy or management level. In all these processes, there should not be any discrimination against women either in perception, feelings, communication or action.

Managerial performance is the outcome of three major variables: (1) individual (human); (2) social (human); and (3) non-human. So for effective performance a person must have the necessary abilities, skills, proper motivation and the necessary traits which suit the job requirement (whether inborn or acquired). The major factors which determine the career decision is the ambition/aspirations, interest, and determination whether for a man or woman. Once this is instilled, people can be trained for the various skills/abilities appropriate for the jobs. The different skills to be developed are human skills, task skills and conceptual skills.

People with high motivation and task orientation and organisational goal orientation perform an effective job in management. Women are basically task oriented and they are sensitive to the needs of the organisation. But what is lacking is the conceptual skills and the decisive nature. Once the proper exposure to the various situations is given, they are able to develop the ability to do the job. The predisposition to think, act and feel positively towards an organisational goal is a very important prerequisite. It is only the intrinsic rewards which lead to higher performance. The most immediate motivational determinant of task performance is the subject's goals. Moreover, higher the intended level of achievement, higher is the level of performance.

In the case of women, primary consideration should be given to personality development, since many of them are not exposed to an environment congenial for effective development in this domain. When you are exposed to the macro environment, the requirements to interact in that context, develop the confidence required for a particular job. If self actualisation is a need to be identified by women, they would express their behaviour and actions to promote that ideal. Extrinsic factors like pay and job security would be only relevant in the lower socio-economic strata where financial aspects have to be given priority. Women of today want positions of authority and they want to make a contribution to the organisation through positions of authority.

The general attitude towards women administrators seems to be favourable although few respondents felt that the employee morale and efficiency are affected to some extent with women administrators. Men respondents also expressed their view of working comfortably with female administrators. Some of the women respondents also felt very comfortable working with male bosses. Many women respondents felt that women bosses place extra demands on them which may be difficult to cope up at times. Women by and large are task oriented and would feel more responsible for moulding their subordinates into competent administrators.

Although today's male administrators are willing to accept the idea that women desire and should have an equal chance to succeed, still many think that a woman must be exceptional to succeed. Consequently a woman has to work twice as hard as compared to a man, to succeed. If people expect greater expectation from women compared to men in spite of her familial roles and constraints, many women who have managerial potential but do not strike others as being exceptional may never be given the opportunity they deserve, to demonstrate their abilities. Surprisingly most of the respondents agree to the statement that men and women should follow the same career path if their capabilities are equal. This causes a contradicting situation. If more women have to succeed in educational administration, there are some essential considerations to be made at the governmental, organisational, technological and individual family level.

Governmental Level

There is need for creation of appropriate opportunities through properly directed programmes of action. These benefits should be available to the middle and lower socio-economic strata of the society. Policy decisions should be made to bring women into the mainstream of national development. Along with the policy decision, machinery for effective implementation also should be planted. Educational and career opportunities for women should form part of deliberate governmental decisions and national priorities. There is need for a comprehensive nationwide strategy and a governmental plan of action that can make women fully realise their potential and opportunities in all spheres of national development.

Organisational Level

Every organisation needs to develop a culture for its development. It must have its own cultural norms that constitute what is expected, supported and accepted ways of behaving. They influence everyone's perceptions, values and attitudes, which indicate the direction in which organisations are likely to move in the future. The role of each employee in the organisation and also the status of women employees in the organisation is determined to a great extent by the organisational perception. In the organisational setup, the male scepticism about the progress of women administrators has to be eliminated. Instead, facilitating factors have to be promoted for women to stay in the job. Basically the attitudes towards women in the work place have to be positive acknowledging their talents and capabilities. Recruitment policy has to be objective to match the organisational goals and individual's potentials and capabilities.

Considering the organisational structure and functions in relation to the governmental policies, one has to arrive at a formula of work load for women in organisations with due considerations of her familial roles she has to play during the crucial years of child bearing and rearing. All women in the expanding stage of family cycle should be assisted by evolving personal policies for involving women by having flexible rules, preferential treatment and adequate opportunities of close by housing facilities, creches etc. Those women absorbed in a job during the expanding stage of family life cycle should preferably be on half time basis since she is required to give full time attention to the home and family. By adopting such a policy, she is able to get back into the mainstream of development as and when she can afford to give greater inputs and at the same time give opportunity to all other incumbents for the job. For women to be able to get back in full swing to the jobs of their abilities and choice, there has to be in-service training programmes which will bring them back into the mainstream. The government and the organisations should work in co-ordination for organising the in-service programmes.

Technological Level
Technological developments have changed our life style. They change the environments and the forms of available goods and services; thus influencing the family and other social systems. Increased mechanical help, creche services, convenient foods, convenient transport system and housing facilities should be made available to the women when they go out for work. If technology can help women to do some part of the work at home, it would help women a great deal.

In the organisational setup also, the technological advancement can facilitate management functions especially information processing. The procedure could be simplified to eliminate the paper work considerably. Computers when used in admissions, time tabling and examinations, simplify a lot of work and accurate information would be available when it is needed.

Individual Family Level
Socialisation of children to gear themselves to suitable aspiration is important especially for a female child. In order to make this happen in our society there should be special programmes for parents and community at large and also teachers of the pre primary, primary and secondary schools for initiating them into the right career decisions regardless of the role script specifications followed traditionally. Some role adjustment pattern has to be evolved and nurtured from early

childhood. If sex stereotyping is not done from the early years it would be a natural growth for boys and girls to think and direct themselves according to their abilities and potentials.

Women have been often held back because of their preconceived ideas about the priority of roles they have to fulfil. The familial roles become very important for women and reinforce their dependent attitudes and they turn to only familial role fulfilment. With the aspirations they have started in their career and the ability and the training they have nurtured over the years, many sit back at home doing very little even when the children have become old enough to take care of themselves. This creates stresses and pressures, both psychological and physical. This is one area where help is needed to resolve conflicts in themselves so that career could be seen as a rational decision regardless of familial situations they are placed in.

4.1 Implications for Training
Self Development

The present study showed that there are no significant differences between men and women once they reach the level of senior administrators. Both men and women are capable and have the potential for effective management. The requirements for effective administrators according to the respondents include:

— ability to deal with the people
— clarity of objectives
— effective communication
— ability to accept criticism and
— ability to listen

Besides this, administrators have the basic awareness about personal growth, self motivation, alertness for self development, sense of integrity, concern for values, actions, orientations, concern for self respect, judgement for situational appropriateness, task orientation, pursuit of knowledge, an

Conclusions

aptitude for innovative thinking and endeavour to derive satisfaction from job. Therefore training programmes should focus on the self development to have high and rising aspirations and self esteem. They have to be sufficiently motivated to achievement and highly committed to the organisation.

There is strong need to re-educate the administrators to suit the developmental needs and understand the significance of team work. Attitude towards the work manifests itself in the feeling of complacence, challenge and motivation. Many people are inclined towards complaisance because of certain environmental factors. An individual has to examine these factors critically in order to rescue his/her basic instinct of challenge and innovation which would enhance his/her capacity to perform.

Management Process

Many respondents pointed out the need for training in:

(1) Planning, implementing, monitoring and evaluating management process.
(2) Identification of constraints and opportunities and planning towards long-term development.
(3) Decision making.
(4) Time management with special reference to time wasters and savers.
(5) Financial managements.
(6) Principles, tools and techniques for efffective management.
(7) Evaluation and auditing progress to identify her/his perceived potential with reference to what she/he possesses. The application of potential is a direct function of an individual's effort and intrinsic motivation which can be closely watched and geared in a positive direction.
(8) Confidence building, communication skills and assertive training, conflict resolution, negotiation etc.
(9) Training for men and women in the family and also in

educational institution with reference to:

— career aspirations
— curriculum opportunities and
— role scripts (socialisation to avoid sex bias for any profession).

(10) Coping with problems and stress and be able to work in harmony regardless of gender.
(11) Male administrators need to have additional training in dealing with people, listening to people, adopting ways of evaluation and accepting criticism. They also need to be more flexible and able to communicate effectively.
(12) Female administrators need to adopt more flexible management styles and this must be general administrative skills, with special emphasis on assertion, confidence and decision making skills.
(13) There is a need to strengthen the positive qualities of women like persuasion, caring and sharing and also hearing the other side patiently.
(14) Women need training in co-operative and collaborative management.

Other Factors

Besides training in self-development and management process, administrators need to be aware of the constraints from the environment and how the same could be converted to opportunities so that they could achieve the maximum possible development in line with their potentials.

1. There is felt need to have a shift from administrative procedures, rules and regulations mainly restrictive, inhibiting and over protective by nature to an efficient management system where administrators can manage the resources and talent with encouragement and trust. The present atmosphere of overcentralisation of

policy and its implementation should give way to policy, only in broad terms and implementation left to the second line and junior level administration.
2. A large number of reports highlighted the subtle encouragement to women aspirants for positions of authority built in our system. There is apparently a basic double standard latent in our educational system. A legitimate feminine perspective should exist as a healthy parallel to the dominant male role, and it must be integrated into all our systems, if women are to be involved in the growth and progress of the country.
3. Women should be encouraged to participate in educational administration by way of offering suitable curriculum, providing opportunities for entry into the job's situation and also opportunities for advancement. These can be achieved only if we provide suitable working hours, management training for resource use especially time and energy, role adjustment providing incentives or facilities offering family support, apropriate socialisation for girls to become career minded and providing residence close to place of work and providing the cultural and financial support.

One other important factor which we should stress in our society is the socialisation of girls and boys in the family. Boys from the start of their career, identify ultimate goals and work out the various steps and stages necessary to achieve these goals, while girls tend to wait and see what happens before committing themselves to long-term programmes or aspirations. This would clearly be linked to the unknown consequences of marriage for most women and the interruption of child rearing and subsequent roles. Some studies indicate that a third of women entering graduate courses showed no reason for entering college.

The family and the school socialise girls into sex roles leading to work commitment and fluctuating career patterns. Even after successful completion of the education, they choose jobs only to use their education and training or to do something useful. They had not planned for a specific line of specialisation. This is the reason for the under representation of women in key educational posts in India. The difference in aspirations and planning goes right back to the socialisation stage. Female socialisation systematically brainwashes women into developing a set of personality attributes which make them passive, emotional and dependent. The process of socialisation of individuals is hinged on psychological, social, cultural, economic and organisational factors and essentially consists of proposing to the individual, the stereotype to which she is impelled to conform. The agents in this process are the family, the school and the society as a whole. This socialisation process shapes and moulds certain characteristics which are important to enable women to take up managerial positions. This can be ingrained and developed in them only if the agents of socialisation namely, the family, school, and the society reorient their approach towards women and development. As it is the school that provides the conformist environment, it is the responsibility of the society and the educationists to refashion the education system to further the interests of women and particularly encourage policies designed for enabling women to take to management areas.

4. In formulating policies for women's development and in particular active participation and association of women in higher education, there is a need for a shift in the recognition of women from being regarded as targets of welfare policies in the social sectors to their being regarded as critical groups for development. The country's development is not possible without the

Conclusions

willing and conscious participation of one half of its population, namely, women. Through such participation women should be able to reduce if not overcome the resistance and barriers to equality and development. Another wind of change that is blowing is the new thrust that is being imparted in the development thinking which recognises the importance of economic independence, status, educational freedom and social freedom for women in society. The growth of organised articulation of women's problems by social organisation and revival of social debate on women's issues are so important that Government should come out with strong legislative and institutional support.

It is not sufficient to conceive of development of women in terms of awarding a few more scholarships to encourage them to higher education. What is needed is women's participation in full manner in higher education with the society giving up its patriarchal and hierachial and authoritarian attitude which oppresses and exploits the female segment.

For women, to be actively involved in administration, the major policy making activity should not be the prerogative of only one sex. It is in the national interest that the abilities of women need to be used as well as those of men. If the woman has the extra burden of caring for the family, some policy decision has to be made regarding the equivalent women positions to men positions in an organisation. Because of the continued biological role women have to perform and the unwillingness of men to share household duties, some concessions in work load have to be given for women to do the assigned work effectively and meaningfully.

Bibliography

1. ALNQUIST, E.M. AND ANGRIST, S.S.
   'Role Model Influences in College Women's Career Aspirations,'
   Merril Palmer
   Quarterly of Behaviour and Development, 1971, p17, 263-79.
2. AMATEA, ELLEN, S. AND OTHERS
   'Assessing the Work and Family Role Expectations of Career Oriented Men and Women: the Life Role Salience Scales'
   Journal of Marriage and the Family, 48(4), November 1986, p. 831-838.
3. ANDERSON, J.
   'Psychological Determinations in Women and Success'
   Kuncsen, R. ed. Horrow, 1974.
4. BANDARI ASHOK SINGH, D.V.
   'Factors affecting Productivity of Indian Workmen'.
   --A contextual analysis, *Indian Management*, August 1986, p 17-25.
5. BLUMBERG, R.L. AND DWARAKI, L.
   'India's Educated Women Options and Constraints'
   Hindustan Publishing Corporation, Delhi, 1980.
6. BOULDING, ELISE.
   'Familial Constraints on Women's Work Roles'
   Signs 1:95. 118, 1976.
7. BUTLER, M.W., PARSLEY.
   'Coordinated Career couples: Convergence and Divergence'
   Dual career couples, Beverly Hills, California, 1980, p 287-288.
8. CHATTERJEE, SHOMA, A.
   "Do Women cope better with Stress than Men?'
   Mirror 27(4), February 1988, p 51-56.
9. CLEVERDON, J.
   'Women in Management'
   The Industrial Society, 1980.
10. COOPER, C.L. AND DAVIDSON, M.J.
    'High pressure, working lives of Women Managers'
    Fontana: London, 1982.

Bibliography

11. COOPER, C. (ED.)
    'Practical Approaches to Women's Career Development;'
    Man Power Services Commission, Sheffield, 1982.
12. DAVIDSON, M.J. AND COOPER, C.L.
    'The Extra Pressures on Women Executives'
    Personal Management, 1980 a12, 6, 48-51.
13. DAVIDSON, M.J. AND COOPER, C.L.
    'What Women Managers Face'
    Management Today, 1981, February, p80-83.
14. DAVIS KEITH
    'Human Behaviour at Work'
    5th Editor Tata M.C. Graw Hill Publishing Co. Ltd., New Delhi, 1977.
15. DAVIS LYNN
    'Women in Educational Management and the Third World'
    A comparative framework for analysis
    International J. of Educational Development Vol. 6, No. 1, Birmingham
    10 6 75.
16. DUBLIN, THOMAS
    'Women at Work'
    Columbia University Press, New York, 1975.
17. FELOBERG, ROSYLIN, L. AND GLEN EVELYN, W.
    'Male and Female Job versus Gender'
    Models in the Sociology of Work, Boston University, Boston.
18. FONDA, N. AND PAUL, N.
    'Life/Work Planning Workshops for Women'
    Cooper C.L. (ed)
19. FRETZ, C.F. AND HAYMAN, J.
    'Progress for Women/Men are still more Equal'
    HBR No. 73503, September October.
20. FRIEDAN, BETTY.
    'The Feminine Mystique'
    New York, 1963.
21. GREENGALGH, C.
    'Male and Female Wage Diffferentials in Great Britain Marriage and Equal Opportunity'
    Economic Journal, December 1980.
22. HARTMANN, HEIDI,
    'The Family as the Locus of Gender, Class and Political Struggle'
    The Example of Housework, Signs 6: 366-374.
23. HASANI, MEHRA.
    'Women at Work the position of women in India'
    Bombay Leslu Sawhney Programme of Training for Democracy, 1973.

24. HENRY, M. AND JARDIAN, A.
   'The Management Women'
   Pan Books, London, 1979.
25. HOLTMAN, L.W.
   'The Employment of Women, Education and Fertility in Women' Women and Achievement, Hedrick, M. et al, John Wiley & Sons, London, 1980.
26. HUNT, A.
   'Management Attitudes and Practices towards Women at Work'
   HMSO, London, 1975.
27. 'The Management women in India, a myth or reality'
   Indian Management, August 1986, p 13-16.
28. 'Male Managers' Attitude towards Women at Work'
   Indian Management, January 1985.
29. KAHN HUT, DAMELS, A.R., COLVARD RICHARD
   'Women and Work'
   Oxford University Press, 1982.
30. KAHN, H.R. DANIELS, K.A. AND COLVARD, R.
   'Women, Work, Problems and Perspectives'
   New York, Oxford University Press, 1982.
31. KANTER, M. ROGEBETH.
   'The impact of Hierarchial Structures on the Work Behaviour of Women and Men'
   Vale University.
32. KATZ, D. AND KAHN, R.L.
   'The Social Psychology of Organisations'
   John Willey & Sons. 1966.
33. LAL DAS D. K.
   'Male Managers Attitude towards Women at Work'
   January 1985.
34. LANGRISH, S.V.
   'The training needs of Women and Men Managers'
   EOC/UMIST Conference on Women Managers and positive action Manehas, 1983.
35. LANGRISH, S.V. AND SMITH, J.M.
   'Women in Management, their Views and Training needs'
   Training Services Division, Man power Services Commission, 1979.
36. LARWOOD, L. AND WOOD, M.M.
   'Women in Management'
   Lamington, Massachusetts, D.C. Herth & Co., 1977.
37. LOCB, J.W, AND FERBER, M.A.
   'Representation Performance Status of Women on the Faculty at the Campus of University of III inois'

Bibliography

38. MACOBY, E.E. AND JACKLEN, C.N.
    'The Psychology of Sex Differences'
    California, Stanford University Press, 1974.
39. MACKENIZIE, R. ALEC.
    'Successful Time Management Methods'
    New Delhi, Vision Books, 1983.
40. MAHAJAN, AMARJIT.
    'Women's Two Roles: A study of Role Conflict'
    Indian Journal of Social Work, January 1966, p 337-380.
41. MINTZBERG, H.
    'The Nature of Managerial Work'
    Narpen & Raul, New York, 1973.
42. MUKHERJI, KARTICK, C.
    'Comparative Study of Some Educational Problems'
    Lalvani Publishing House, Bombay 1972.
43. PANDE MRINAL.
    'Can Tomorrow's Management learn from Women'
    Indian Management, March 1987, p 18-20.
44. PARUK UDAI ET AL.
    'Behavioral Processes in Organisations'
    Oxford and IBH Publishing Co., New Delhi, 1981.
45. RANADI, S.N. AND RAMACHANDRA, P.
    'Women and Employment'
    Tata Institute of Social Sciences, 1970.
46. SCHEIN EAGAR, H.
    'Organisational Psychology'
    Prentice Hall of India Pvt. Ltd., New Delhi, 1969.
47. SMITH MIKE AND WOOD EDDI ET AL.
    'A Development Programme for Women in Management'
    Gower Publishing Co. Ltd., Gower House, Hampshire, U.K. 1985.
48. SUTTON, D.C. AND MOORE, K.K.
    'Executive Women, 20 years later'
    Business Review, September October 5: 1985, p 42.
49. U.G.C. REPORT 1982.
50. VARGHESE, M.A. AND KHANNA, G.
    'Indian Women Today'
    Vikas Publishing House Pvt. Ltd., New Delhi, 1978.
51. Y.W.C.A.
    'The Educated Women in the Indian Society Today'
    Tata H.C. Graw Hill Publishing Co. Ltd., Bombay, New Delhi. 1971.

Distributed By
ADVENT BOOKS,
141 East 44 Street
New York, NY 10017